Stereoph

performance and

CW00371424

GUITAR
TAB
EDITION

£12.95

polygram music publishing limited

exclusive distributors:
music sales limited
8/9 frith street
london w1v 5tz
england
music sales pty limited
120 rothschild avenue
rosebery nsw 2018
australia

order no.am957077
isbn 0-7119-7319-9
this book © copyright 1999 by
polygram music publishing limited
www.musicsales.com

music arranged by james dean
(except she takes her clothes off,
arranged by hussein boon)
music processed by digital music art

printed in the united kingdom by
printwise limited, haverhill, suffolk

your guarantee of quality:
as publishers, we strive to produce every
book to the highest commercial standards

whilst endeavouring to retain the
original running order of the recorded album,
the book has been carefully designed to
minimise awkward page turns and to make playing
from it a real pleasure

particular care has been given to
specifying acid-free, neutral-sized paper
made from pulps which have not been
elemental chlorine bleached

this pulp is from farmed sustainable
forests and was produced with special
regard for the environment

throughout, the printing and binding have
been planned to ensure a sturdy, attractive
publication which should give years of
enjoyment

if your copy fails to meet our high standards,
please inform us and we will gladly replace it

music sales' complete catalogue describes
thousands of titles and is available in full
colour sections by subject, direct from
music sales limited

please state your areas of interest and send
a cheque/postal order for £1.50 for postage to:
music sales limited, newmarket road,
bury st. edmunds, suffolk ip33 3yb

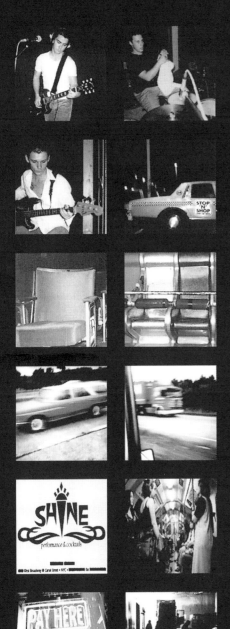

guitar tablature explained

Guitar music can be notated three different ways: on a musical stave, in tablature, and in rhythm slashes

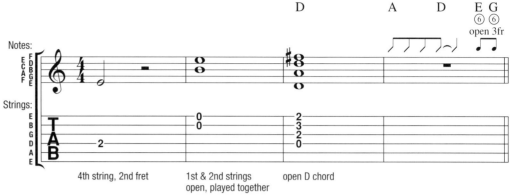

RHYTHM SLASHES are written above the stave. Strum chords in the rhythm indicated. Round noteheads indicate single notes.

THE MUSICAL STAVE shows pitches and rhythms and is divided by lines into bars. Pitches are named after the first seven letters of the alphabet.

TABLATURE graphically represents the guitar fingerboard. Each horizontal line represents a string, and each number represents a fret.

4th string, 2nd fret   1st & 2nd strings open, played together   open D chord

definitions for special guitar notation

SEMI-TONE BEND: Strike the note and bend up a semi-tone (1/2 step).

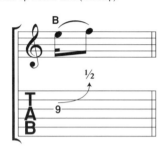

WHOLE-TONE BEND: Strike the note and bend up a whole-tone (whole step).

GRACE NOTE BEND: Strike the note and bend as indicated. Play the first note as quickly as possible.

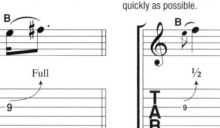

QUARTER-TONE BEND: Strike the note and bend up a 1/4 step.

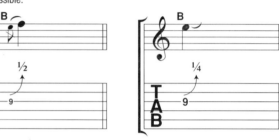

BEND & RELEASE: Strike the note and bend up as indicated, then release back to the original note.

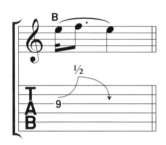

COMPOUND BEND & RELEASE: Strike the note and bend up and down in the rhythm indicated.

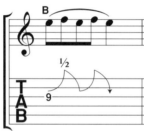

PRE-BEND: Bend the note as indicated, then strike it.

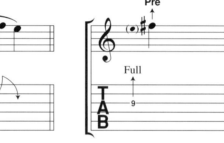

PRE-BEND & RELEASE: Bend the note as indicated. Strike it and release the note back to the original pitch.

UNISON BEND: Strike the two notes simultaneously and bend the lower note up to the pitch of the higher.

BEND & RESTRIKE: Strike the note and bend as indicated then restrike the string where the symbol occurs.

BEND, HOLD AND RELEASE: Same as bend and release but hold the bend for the duration of the tie.

BEND AND TAP: Bend the note as indicated and tap the higher fret while still holding the bend.

VIBRATO: The string is vibrated by rapidly bending and releasing the note with the fretting hand.

HAMMER-ON: Strike the first (lower) note with one finger, then sound the higher note (on the same string) with another finger by fretting it without picking.

PULL-OFF: Place both fingers on the notes to be sounded, Strike the first note and without picking, pull the finger off to sound the second (lower) note.

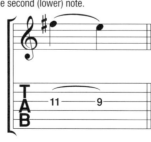

LEGATO SLIDE (GLISS): Strike the first note and then slide the same fret-hand finger up or down to the second note. The second note is not struck.

NOTE: The speed of any bend is indicated by the music notation and tempo.

SHIFT SLIDE (GLISS & RESTRIKE): Same as legato slide, except the second note is struck.

TRILL: Very rapidly alternate between the notes indicated by continuously hammering on and pulling off.

TAPPING: Hammer ("tap") the fret indicated with the pick-hand index or middle finger and pull off to the note fretted by the fret hand.

PICK SCRAPE: The edge of the pick is rubbed down (or up) the string, producing a scratchy sound.

 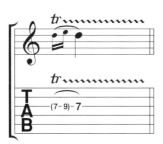 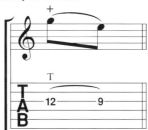 

MUFFLED STRINGS: A percussive sound is produced by laying the fret hand across the string(s) without depressing, and striking them with the pick hand.

NATURAL HARMONIC: Strike the note while the fret-hand lightly touches the string directly over the fret indicated.

PINCH HARMONIC: The note is fretted normally and a harmonic is produced by adding the edge of the thumb or the tip of the index finger of the pick hand to the normal pick attack.

HARP HARMONIC: The note is fretted normally and a harmonic is produced by gently resting the pick hand's index finger directly above the indicated fret (in parentheses) while the pick hand's thumb or pick assists by plucking the appropriate string.

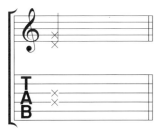   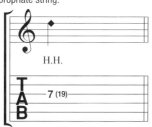

PALM MUTING: The note is partially muted by the pick hand lightly touching the string(s) just before the bridge.

RAKE: Drag the pick across the strings indicated with a single motion.

TREMOLO PICKING: The note is picked as rapidly and continuously as possible.

ARPEGGIATE: Play the notes of the chord indicated by quickly rolling them from bottom to top.

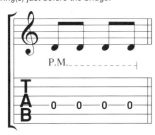 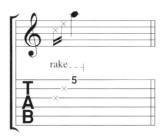  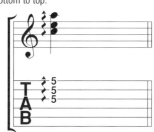

SWEEP PICKING: Rhythmic downstroke and/or upstroke motion across the strings.

VIBRATO DIVE BAR AND RETURN: The pitch of the note or chord is dropped a specific number of steps (in rhythm) then returned to the original pitch.

VIBRATO BAR SCOOP: Depress the bar just before striking the note, then quickly release the bar.

VIBRATO BAR DIP: Strike the note and then immediately drop a specific number of steps, then release back to the original pitch.

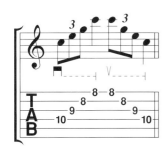 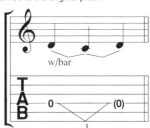

additional musical definitions

 (accent) • Accentuate note (play it louder).

(accent) • Accentuate note with great intensity.

(staccato) • Shorten time value of note.

• Downstroke

V • Upstroke

D.%. al Coda

D.C. al Fine

tacet

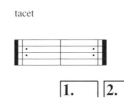

1. **2.**

• Go back to the sign (%), then play until the bar marked *To Coda* ⊕ then skip to the section marked ⊕ *Coda*.

• Go back to the beginning of the song and play until the bar marked *Fine* (end).

• Instrument is silent (drops out).

• Repeat bars between signs.

• When a repeated section has different endings, play the first ending only the first time and the second ending only the second time.

NOTE: Tablature numbers in parentheses mean:
1. The note is sustained, but a new articulation (such as hammer on or slide) begins.
2. A note may be fretted but not necessarily played.

présentation de la tablature de guitare

Il existe trois façons différentes de noter la musique pour guitare : à l'aide d'une portée musicale, de tablatures ou de barres rythmiques.

Les BARRES RYTHMIQUES sont indiquées au-dessus de la portée. Jouez les accords dans le rythme indiqué. Les notes rondes indiquent des notes réciles.

La PORTÉE MUSICALE indique les notes et rythmes et est divisée en mesures. Cette division est représentée par des lignes. Les notes sont : do, ré, mi, fa, sol, la, si.

La PORTÉE EN TABLATURE est une représentation graphique des touches de guitare. Chaque ligne horizontale correspond à une corde et chaque chiffre correspond à une case.

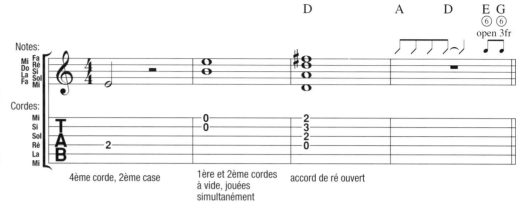

4ème corde, 2ème case   1ère et 2ème cordes à vide, jouées simultanément   accord de ré ouvert

notation spéciale de guitare : définitions

TIRÉ DEMI-TON : Jouez la note et tirez la corde afin d'élever la note d'un demi-ton (étape à moitié).

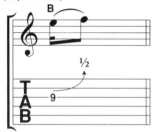

TIRÉ PLEIN : Jouez la note et tirez la corde afin d'élever la note d'un ton entier (étape entière).

TIRÉ D'AGRÉMENT : Jouez la note et tirez la corde comme indiqué. Jouez la première note aussi vite que possible.

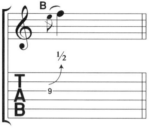

TIRÉ QUART DE TON : Jouez la note et tirez la corde afin d'élever la note d'un quart de ton.

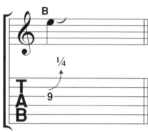

TIRÉ ET LÂCHÉ : Jouez la note et tirez la corde comme indiqué, puis relâchez, afin d'obtenir de nouveau la note de départ.

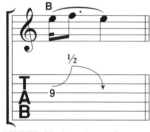

TIRÉ ET REJOUÉ : Jouez la note et tirez la corde comme indiqué puis rejouez la corde où le symbole apparaît.

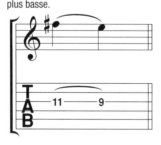

PRÉ-TIRÉ : Tirez la corde comme indiqué puis jouez cette note.

PRÉ-TIRÉ ET LÂCHÉ : Tirez la corde comme indiqué. Jouez la note puis relâchez la corde afin d'obtenir le ton de départ.

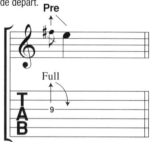

HAMMER-ON: Jouez la première note (plus basse) avec un doigt puis jouez la note plus haute sur la même corde avec un autre doigt, sur le manche mais sans vous servir du médiator.

PULL-OFF: Positionnez deux doigts sur les notes à jouer. Jouez la première note et sans vous servir du médiator, dégagez un doigt pour obtenir la deuxième note, plus basse.

GLISSANDO : Jouez la première note puis faites glisser le doigt le long du manche pour obtenir la seconde note qui, elle, n'est pas jouée.

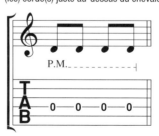

GLISSANDO ET REJOUÉ : Identique au glissando à ceci près que la seconde note est jouée.

HARMONIQUES NATURELLES : Jouez la note tandis qu'un doigt effleure la corde sur le manche correspondant à la case indiquée.

PICK SCRAPE (SCRATCH) : On fait glisser le médiator le long de la corde, ce qui produit un son éraillé.

ÉTOUFFÉ DE LA PAUME : La note est partiellement étouffée par la main (celle qui se sert du médiator). Elle effleure la (les) corde(s) juste au-dessus du chevalet.

CORDES ÉTOUFFÉES : Un effet de percussion produit en posant à plat la main sur le manche sans relâcher, puis en jouant les cordes avec le médiator.

NOTE: La vitesse des tirés est indiquée par la notation musicale et le tempo.

6

erläuterung zur tabulaturschreibweise

Es gibt drei Möglichkeiten, Gitarrenmusik zu notieren: im klassichen Notensystem, in Tabulaturform oder als rhythmische Akzente.

RHYTHMISCHE AKZENTE werden über dem Notensystem notiert. Geschlagene Akkorde werden rhythmisch dargestellt. Ausgeschriebene Noten stellen Einzeltöne dar.

Im **NOTENSYSTEM** werden Tonhöhe und rhythmischer Verlauf festgelegt; es ist durch Taktstriche in Takte unterteilt. Die Töne werden nach den ersten acht Buchstaben des Alphabets benannt.
Beachte: "B" in der anglo-amerkanischen Schreibweise entspricht dem deutschen "H"!

DIE TABULATUR ist die optische Darstellung des Gitarrengriffbrettes. Jeder horizontalen Linie ist eine bestimmte Saite zugeordnet, jede Zahl bezeichnet einen Bund.

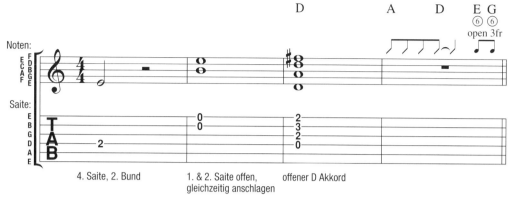

4. Saite, 2. Bund   1. & 2. Saite offen, gleichzeitig anschlagen   offener D Akkord

erklärungen zur speziellen gitarennotation

HALBTON-ZIEHER: Spiele die Note und ziehe dann um einen Halbton höher (Halbtonschritt).

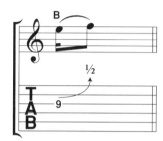

GANZTON-ZIEHER: Spiele die Note und ziehe dann einen Ganzton höher (Ganztonschritt).

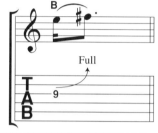

ZIEHER MIT VORSCHLAG: Spiele die Note und ziehe wie notiert. Spiele die erste Note so schnell wie möglich.

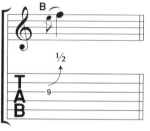

VIERTELTON-ZIEHER: Spiele die Note und ziehe dann einen Viertelton höher (Vierteltonschritt).

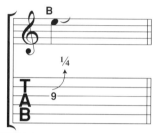

ZIEHEN UND ZURÜCKGLEITEN: Spiele die Note und ziehe wie notiert; lasse den Finger dann in die Ausgangsposition zurückgleiten. Dabei wird nur die erste Note angeschlagen.

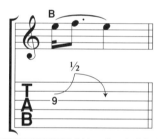

ZIEHEN UND NOCHMALIGES ANSCHLAGEN: Spiele die Note und ziehe wie notiert, schlage die Saite neu an, wenn das Symbol "▶" erscheint und lasse den Finger dann zurückgleiten.

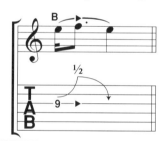

ZIEHER VOR DEM ANSCHLAGEN: Ziehe zuerst die Note wie notiert; schlage die Note dann an.

ZIEHER VOR DEM ANSCHLAGEN MIT ZURÜCKGLEITEN: Ziehe die Note wie notiert; schlage die Note dann an und lasse den Finger auf die Ausgangslage zurückgleiten.

AUFSCHLAGTECHNIK: Schlage die erste (tiefere) Note an; die höhere Note (auf der selben Saite) erklingt durch kräftiges Aufschlagen mit einem anderen Finger der Griffhand.

ABZIEHTECHNIK: Setze beide Finger auf die zu spielenden Noten und schlage die erste Note an. Ziehe dann (ohne nochmals anzuschlagen) den oberen Finger der Griffhand seitlich - abwärts ab, um die zweite (tiefere) Note zum klingen zu bringen.

GLISSANDOTECHNIK: Schlage die erste Note an und rutsche dann mit dem selben Finger der Griffhand aufwärts oder abwärts zur zweiten Note. Die zweite Note wird nicht angeschlagen.

GLISSANDOTECHNIK MIT NACHFOLGENDEM ANSCHLAG: Gleiche Technik wie das gebundene Glissando, jedoch wird die zweite Note angeschlagen.

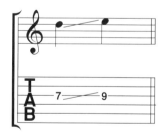

NATÜRLICHES FLAGEOLETT: Berühre die Saite über dem angegebenen Bund leicht mit einem Finger der Griffhand. Schlage die Saite an und lasse sie frei schwingen.

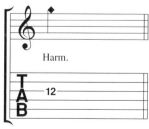

PICK SCRAPE: Fahre mit dem Plektrum nach unten über die Saiten - klappt am besten bei umsponnenen Saiten.

DÄMPFEN MIT DER SCHLAGHAND: Lege die Schlaghand oberhalb der Brücke leicht auf die Saite(n).

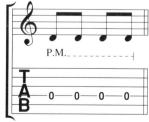

DÄMPFEN MIT DER GRIFFHAND: Du erreichst einen percussiven Sound, indem du die Griffhand leicht über die Saiten legst (ohne diese herunterzudrücken) und dann mit der Schlaghand anschlägst.

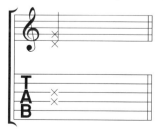

AMMERKUNG: Das Tempo der Zieher und Glissandos ist abhängig von der rhythmischen Notation und dem Grundtempo.

spiegazioni di tablatura per chitarra

La musica per chitarra può essere annotata in tre diversi modi: sul pentagramma, in tablatura e in taglio ritmico

IL TAGLIO RITMICO è scritto sopra il pentagramma. Percuotere le corde al ritmo indicato. Le teste arrotondate delle note indicano note singole.

IL PENTAGRAMMA MUSICALE mostra toni e ritmo ed è divisa da linee in settori. I toni sono indicati con le prime sette lettere dell'alfabeto.

LA TABLATURA rappresenta graficamente la tastiera della chitarra. Ogni linea orizzontale rappresenta una corda, ed ogni corda rappresenta un tasto.

4° corda, 2° tasto   1° e 2° corda aperte, suonate insieme   accordo D aperto

definizioni per annotazioni speciali per chitarra

SEMI-TONO CURVATO: percuotere la nota e curvare di un semitono (1/2 passo).

TONO CURVATO: Percuotere la nota e curvare di un tono (passo intero).

NOTA BREVE, CURVATA: percuotere la nota e curvare come indicato. Suonare la prima nota il più velocemente possibile.

QUARTO DI TONO, CURVATO: Percuotere la nota e curvare di un quarto di passo.

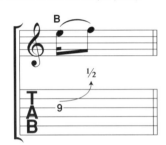

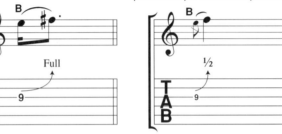
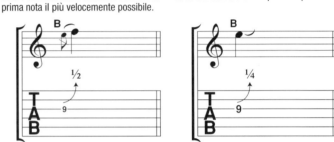

CURVA E LASCIA: Percuotere la nota e curvare come indicato, quindi rilasciare indietro alla nota originale.

CURVA E RIPERCUOTI: Percuotere la nota e curvare come indicato poi ripercuotere la corda nel punto del simbolo.

PRE-CURVA: Curvare la nota come indicato e quindi percuoterla.

PRE-CURVA E RILASCIO: Curvare la nota come indicato. Colpire e rilasciare la nota indietro alla tonalità indicata.

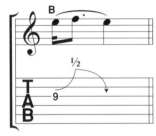
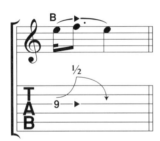
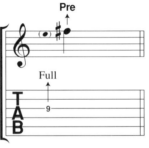

MARTELLO-COLPISCI: Colpire la prima nota (in basso) con un dito; quindi suona la nota più alta (sulla stessa corda) con un altro dito, toccandola senza pizzicare.

TOGLIERE: Posizionare entrambe le dita sulla nota da suonare. Colpire la prima nota e, senza pizzicare, togliere le dita per suonare la seconda nota (più in basso).

LEGATO SCIVOLATO (GLISSATO): Colpire la prima nota e quindi far scivolare lo stesso dito della mano della tastiera su o giù alla seconda nota. La seconda nota non viene colpita.

CAMBIO SCIVOLATO (GLISSARE E RICOLPIRE): Uguale al legato - scivolato eccetto che viene colpita la seconda nota.

ARMONICA NATURALE: Colpire la nota mentre la mano della tastiera tocca leggermente la corda direttamente sopra il tasto indicato.

PIZZICA E GRAFFIA: Il limite del pizzicato è tirato su (o giù) lungo la corda, producendo un suono graffiante.

SORDINA CON IL PALMO: La nota è parzialmente attenuata dalla mano del pizzicato toccando la corda (le corde) appena prima del ponte.

CORDE SMORZATE: Un suono di percussione viene prodotto appoggiando la mano della tastiera attraverso la corda (le corde) senza premere, e colpendole con la mano del pizzicato.

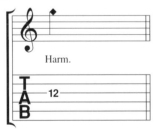

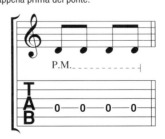
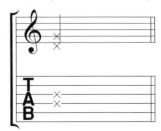

NOTA: La velocità di ogni curvatura è indicata dalle annotazioni musicali e dal tempo.

roll up and shine

words by kelly jones
music by kelly jones, richard jones & stuart cable

at   your -   self?

spit - tin'   fire.

Pre Chorus

So why don't you take a look a - round.

So why don't we take a look in -

- side.

whats a-fraid of.___ It's time___ to breathe,___ time to___ re - lieve,___

it's time___ to shine.___

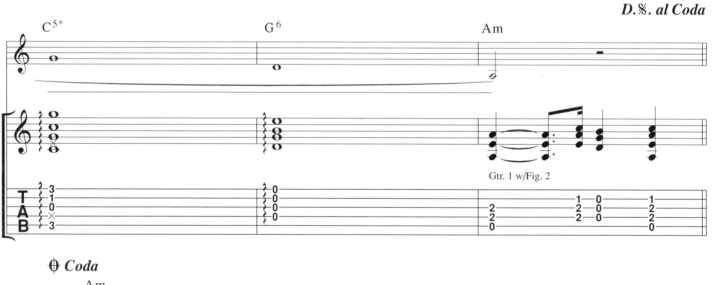

D.%. al Coda

Gtr. 1 w/Fig. 2

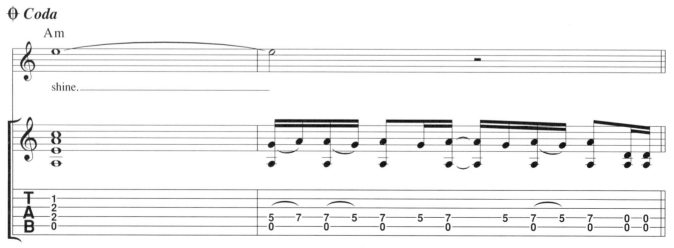

shine.___

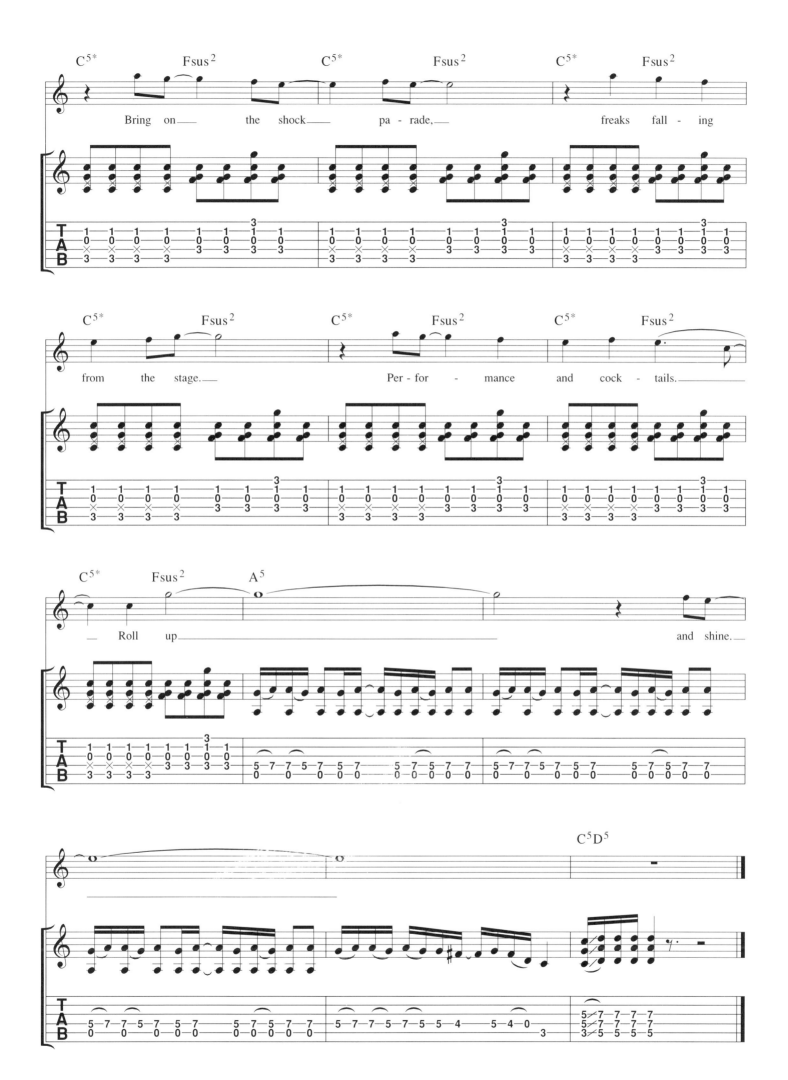

the bartender and the thief

words by kelly jones
music by kelly jones, richard jones & stuart cable

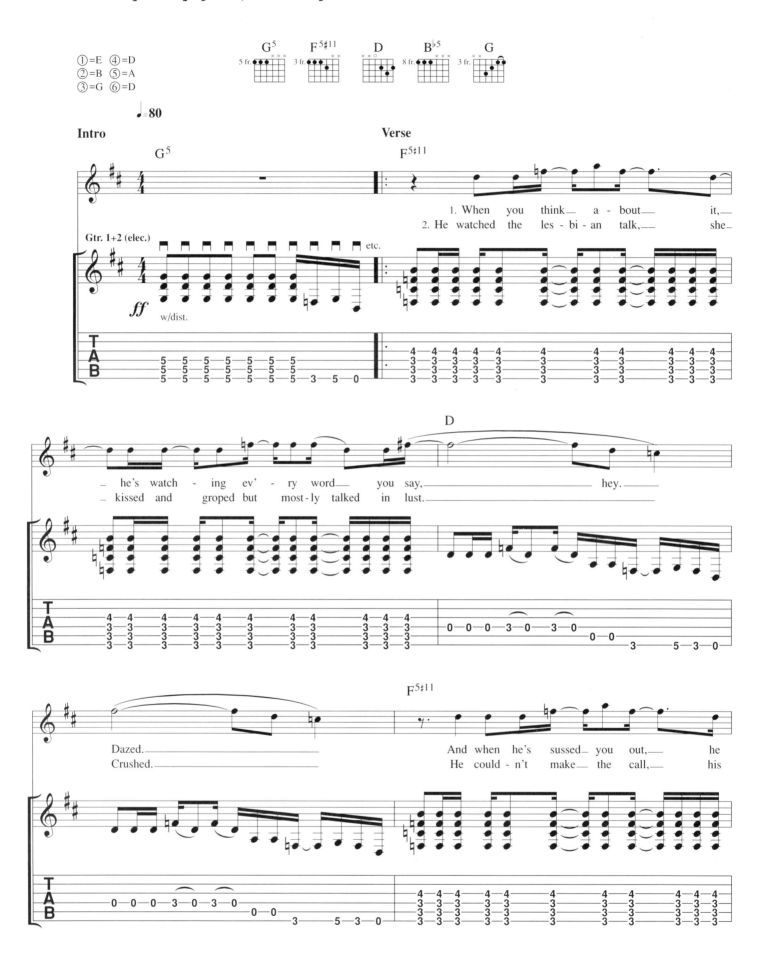

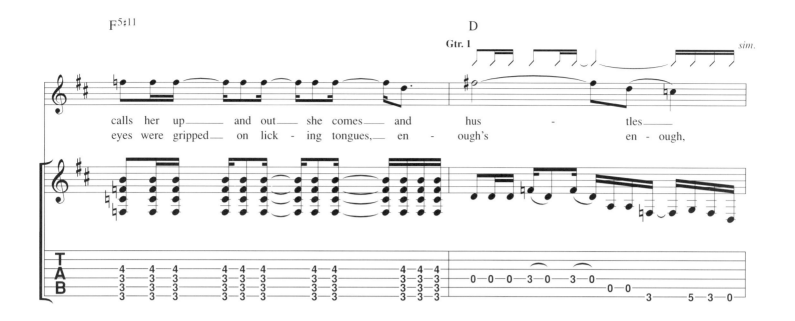

calls her up____ and out____ she comes____ and hus - ____ tles____
eyes were gripped____ on lick - ing tongues,____ en - ough's en - ough,

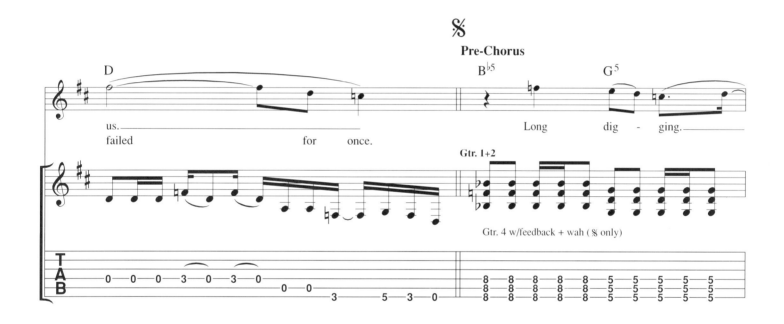

Pre-Chorus

us.____
failed for once.

Long dig - ging.____

Gtr. 4 w/feedback + wah (% only)

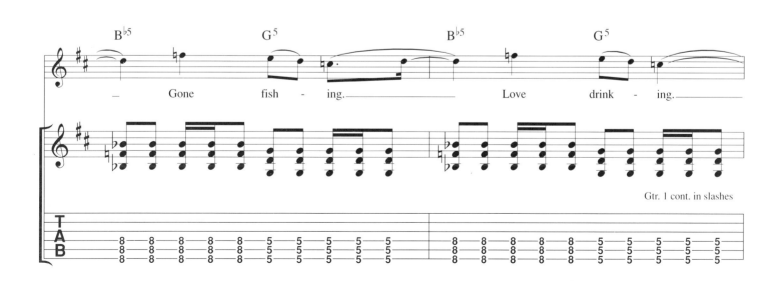

Gone fish - ing.____ Love drink - ing.____

Gtr. 1 cont. in slashes

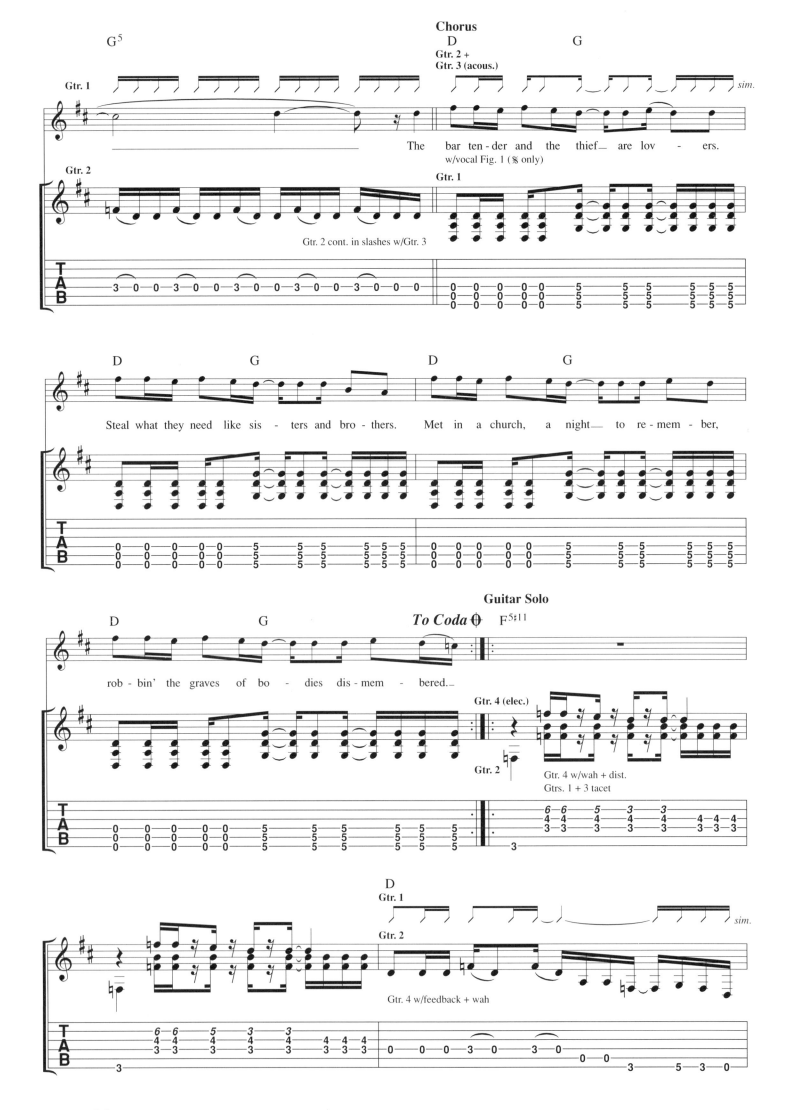

Chorus

The bar ten-der and the thief are lov-ers.

Steal what they need like sis-ters and bro-thers. Met in a church, a night to re-mem-ber,

rob-bin' the graves of bo-dies dis-mem-bered.

Guitar Solo

To Coda

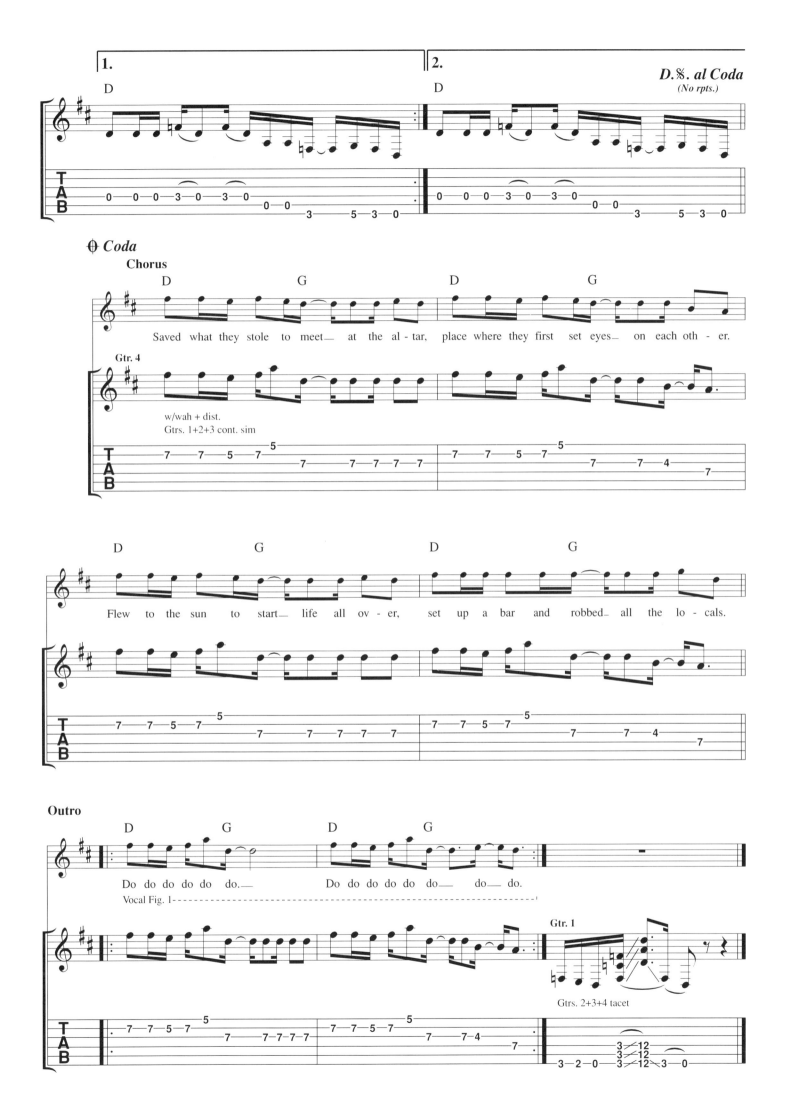

hurry up and wait

words by kelly jones
music by kelly jones, richard jones & stuart cable

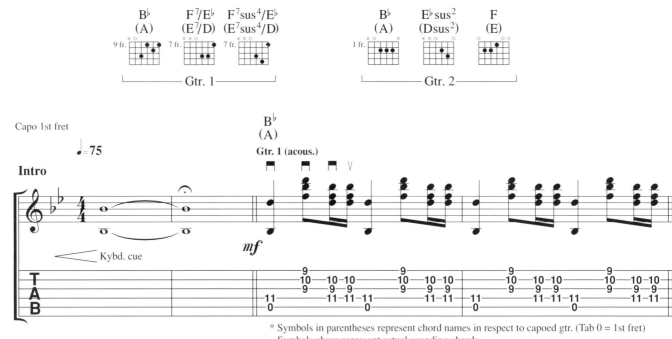

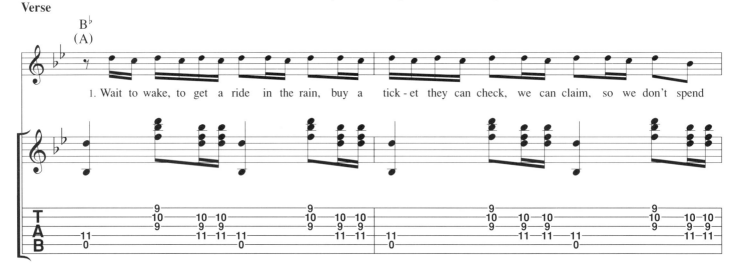

* Symbols in parentheses represent chord names in respect to capoed gtr. (Tab 0 = 1st fret)
Symbols above represent actual sounding chords.

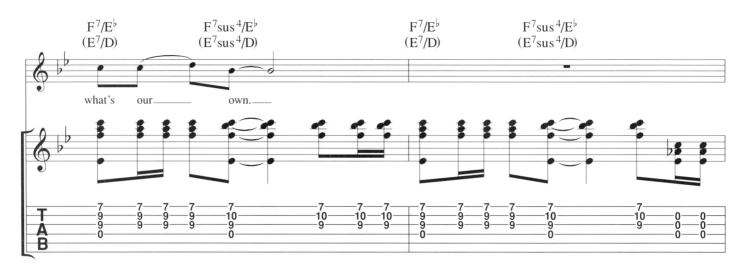

19

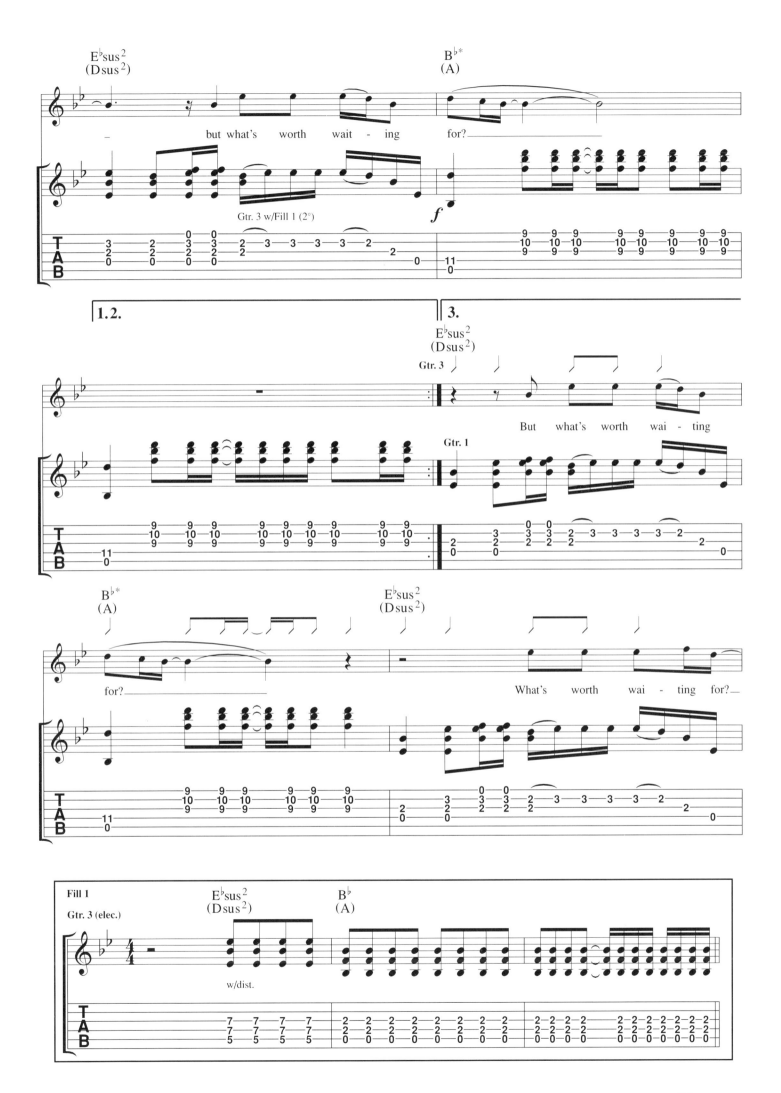

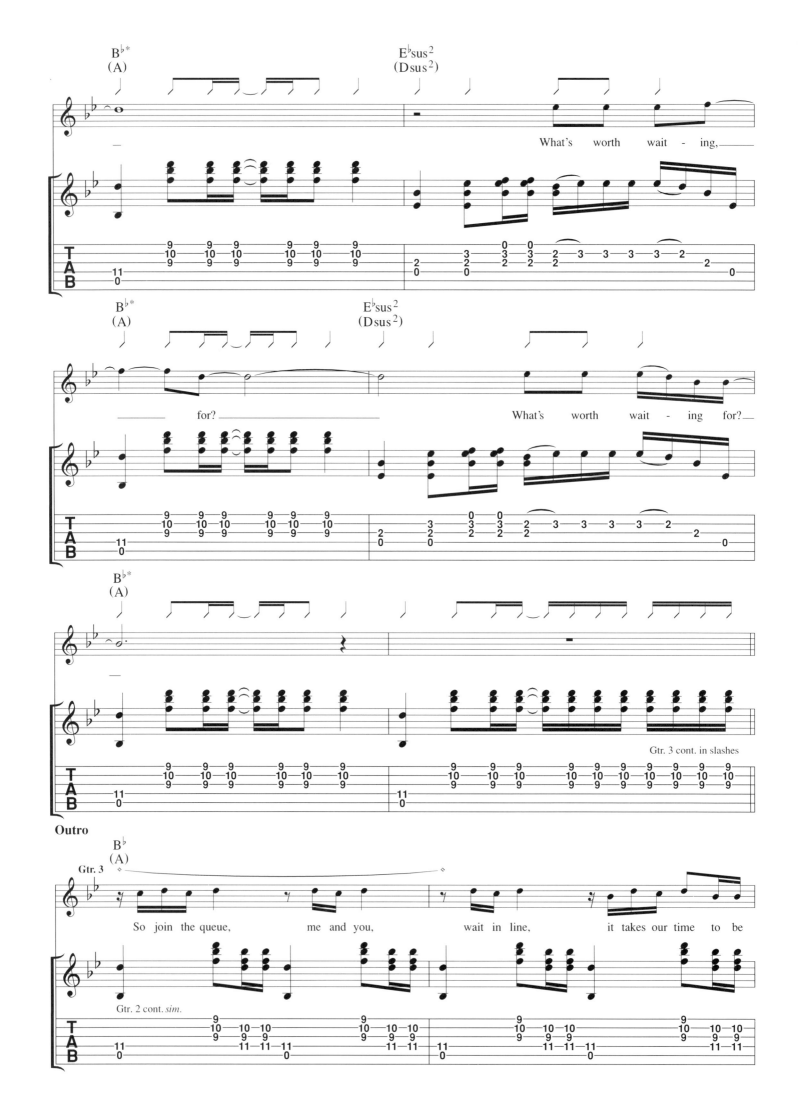

Verse 3:

We wait to get warm, the car starts from cold stall
To make a first move magazines made the rules to make us lose
For your dream man, the house you could both plan, the car in the sales
Add the wet dream with the man you wish that you had.

Verse 4:

A watched pot never boils, sugar seconds to dissolve
Feel your appetite loss, food's relevance lost inside
We wait to get there, and when we get there
We wait around for anyone to tell us what we even got there for.

pick a part that's new

words by kelly jones
music by kelly jones, richard jones & stuart cable

1. I've ne-ver been___ here be-fore,___ did-n't know___ where to go,___
2. Peo- ple drink-ing on their own,___ push but- tons on the phone,___

25

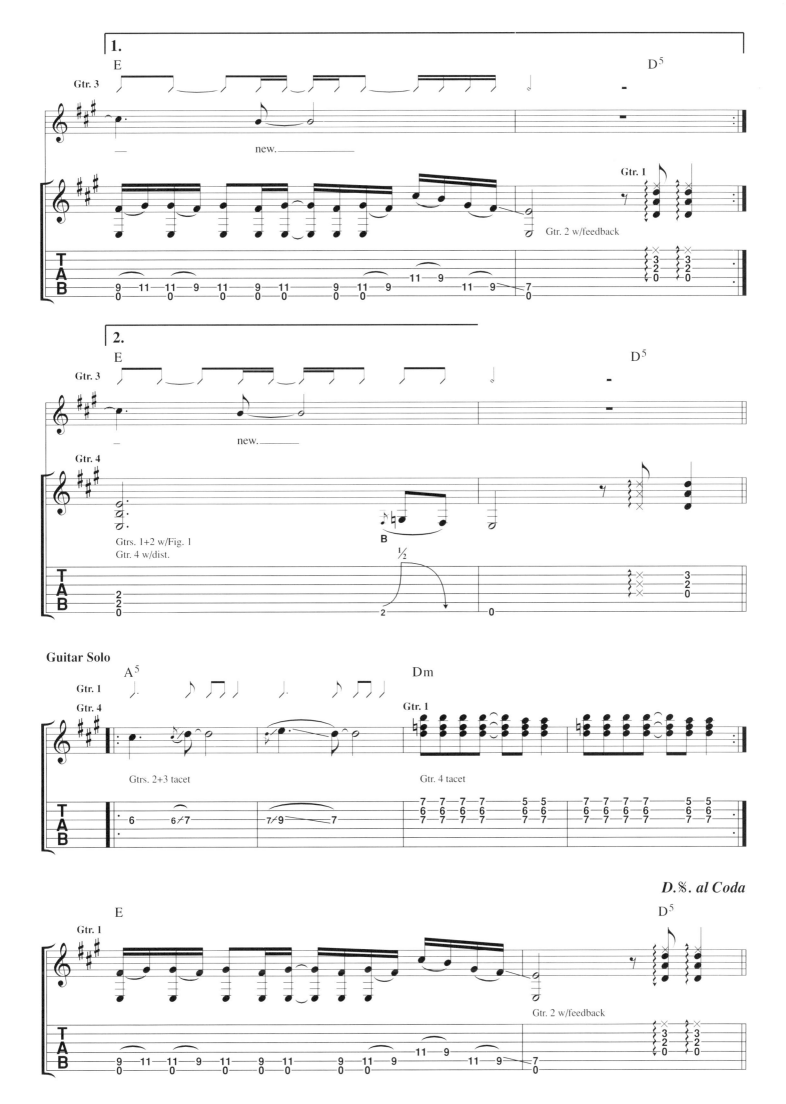

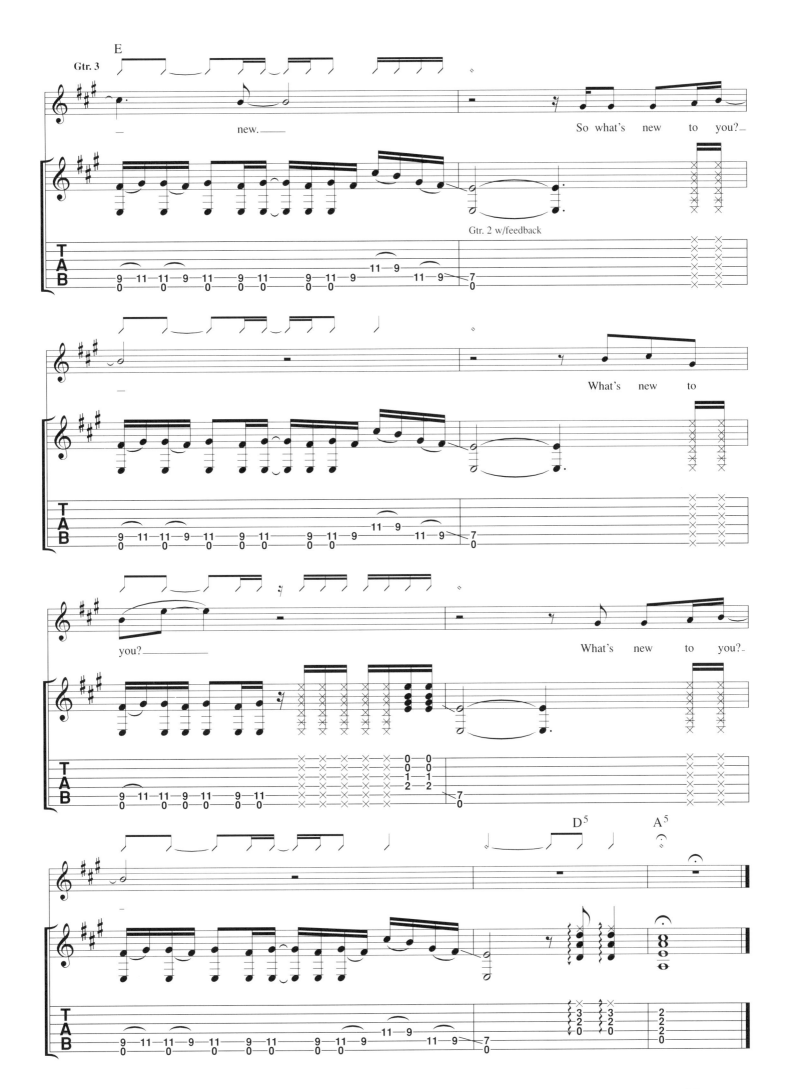

just looking

words by kelly jones
music by kelly jones, richard jones & stuart cable

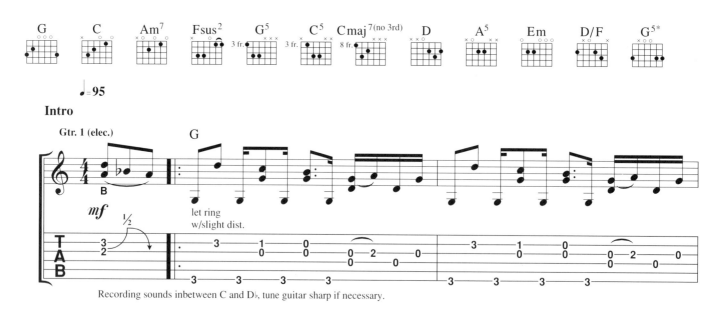

Recording sounds inbetween C and D♭, tune guitar sharp if necessary.

1. There's things I

Verse

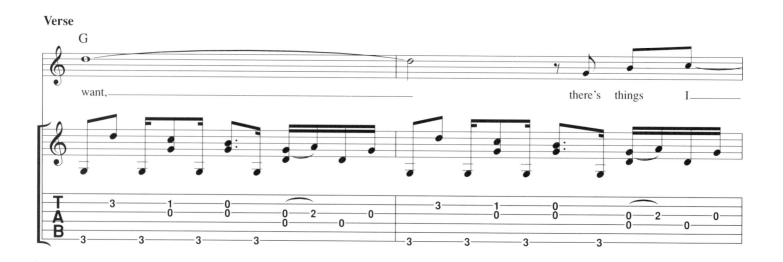

want, there's things I

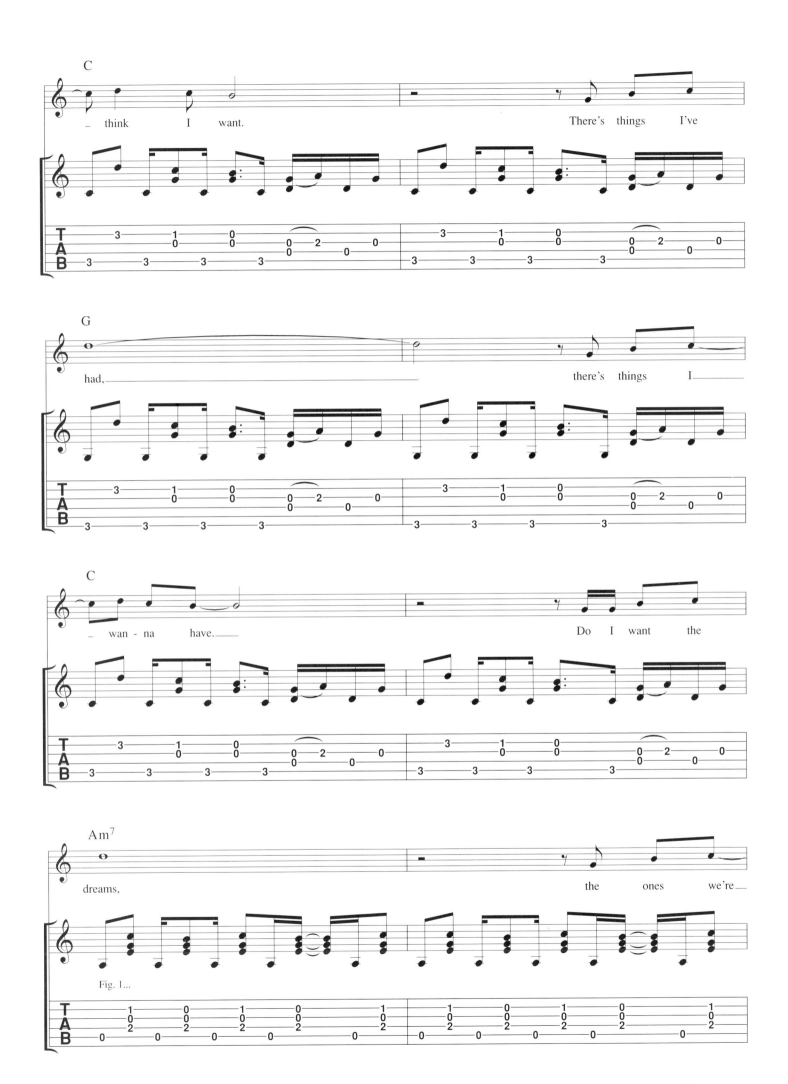

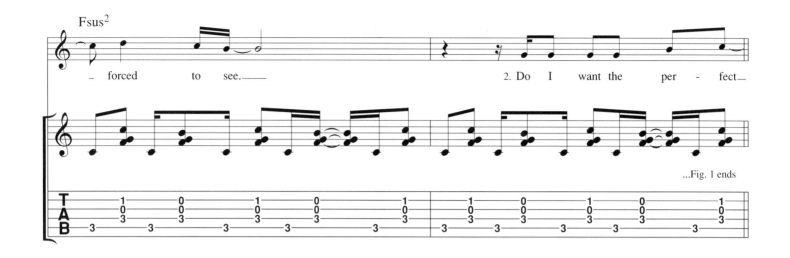

Fsus²

forced to see._____ 2. Do I want the per - fect_____

...Fig. 1 ends

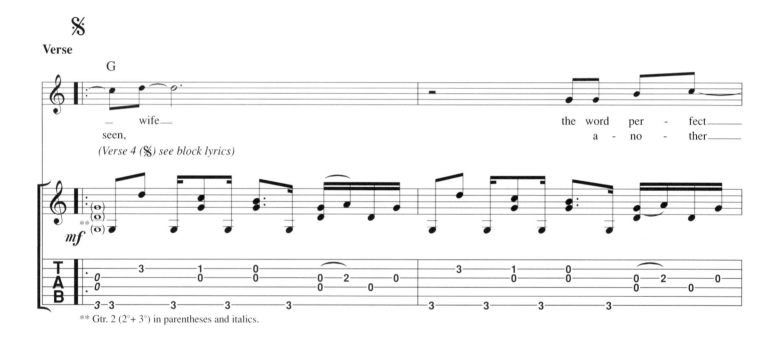

Verse

G

wife_____ the word per - fect_____
seen, a - no - ther_____

(Verse 4 (%) see block lyrics)

mf

** Gtr. 2 (2°+ 3°) in parentheses and italics.

C

ain't_____ quite right, shop - pin' ev - 'ry
could - a' been, you drenched my

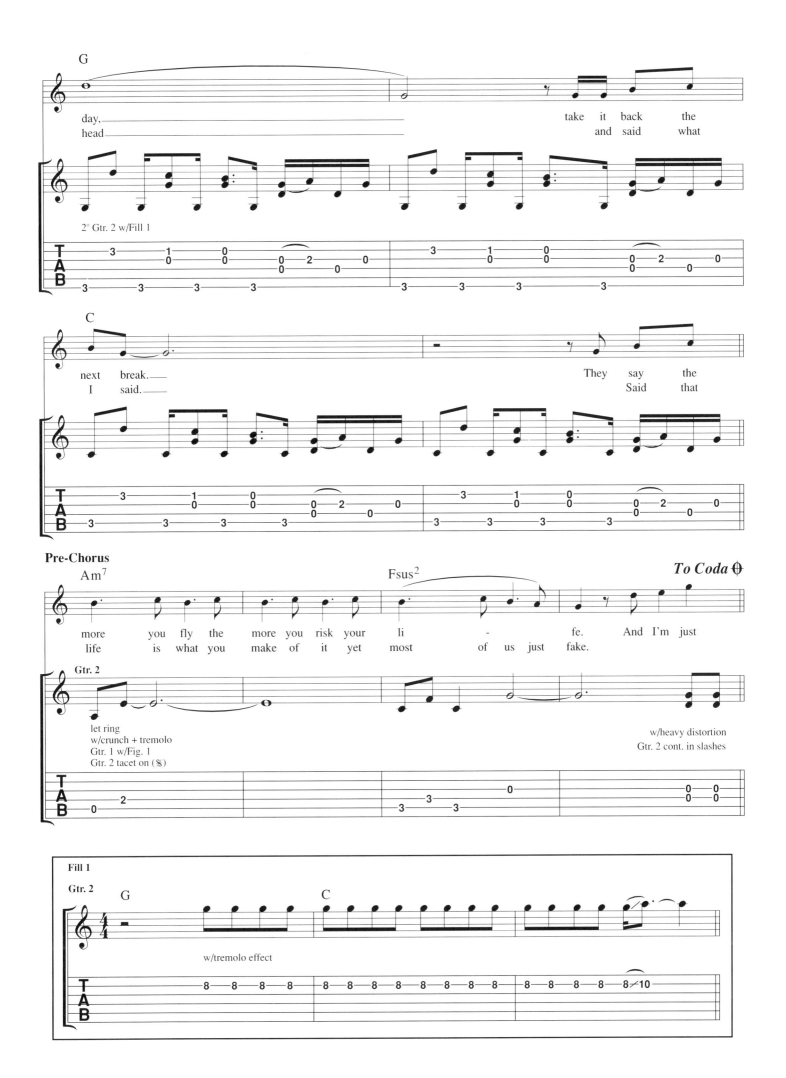

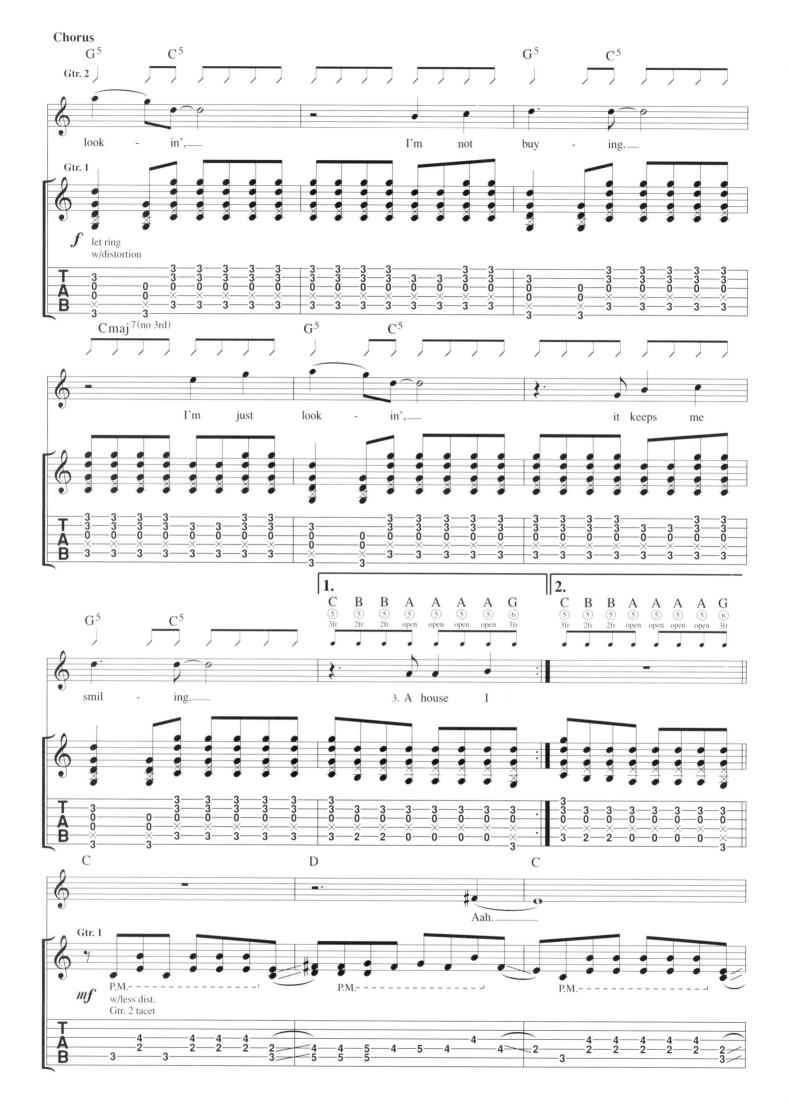

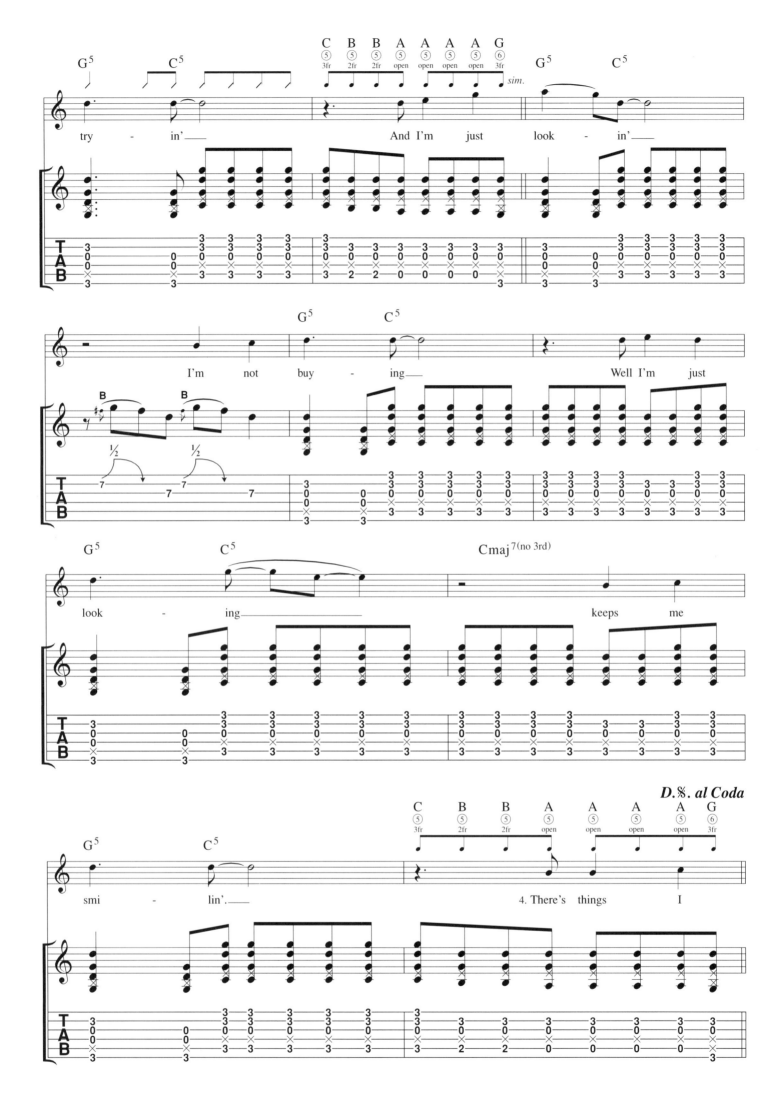

Verse 4 (𝄉):

There's things I want
There's things I think I want.
There's things I've had
There's things I wanna have.
They say the more you fly
The more you risk your life.

half the lies you tell ain't true

words by kelly jones
music by kelly jones, richard jones & stuart cable

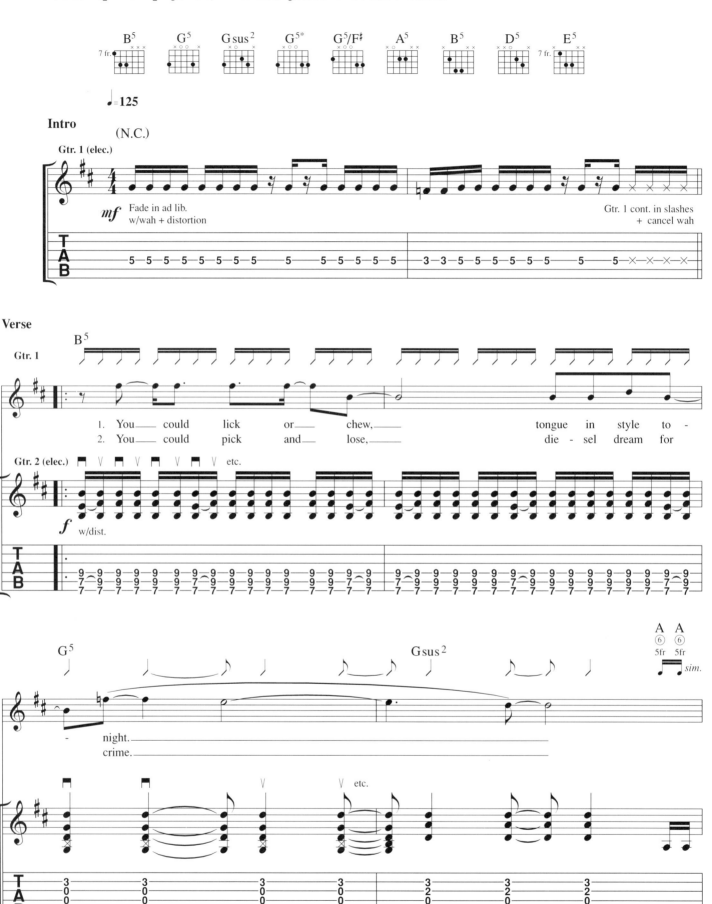

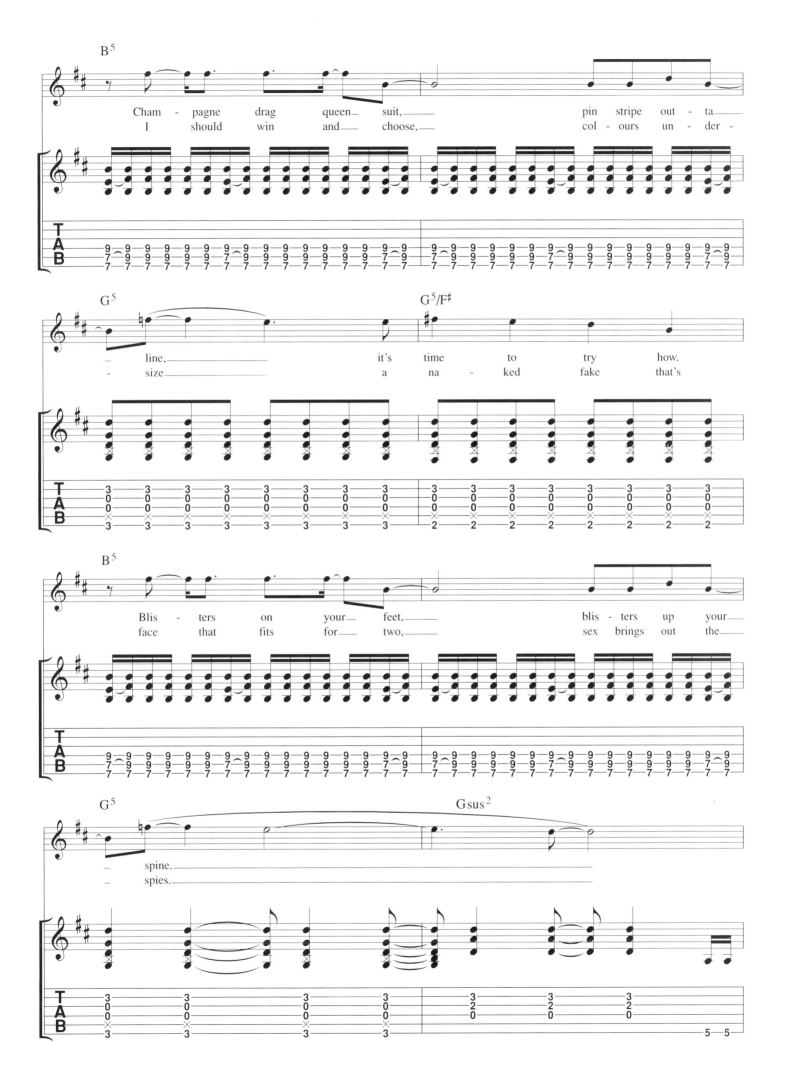

40

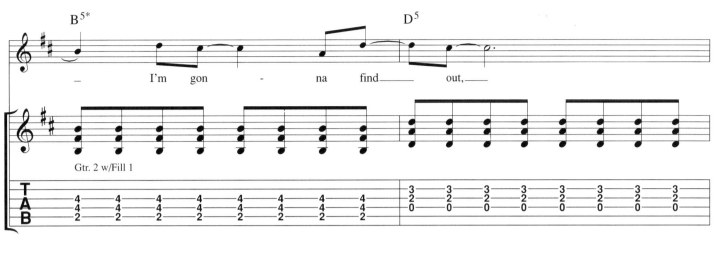

I'm gon - na find_____ out,_____

Gtr. 2 w/Fill 1

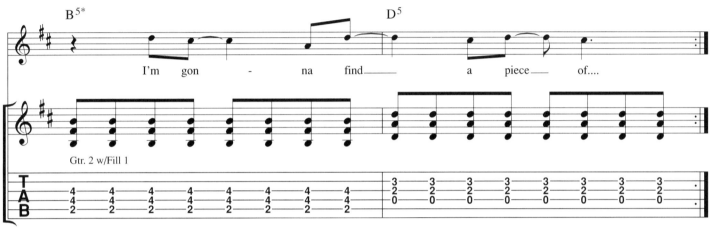

I'm gon - na find_____ a piece_____ of....

Gtr. 2 w/Fill 1

Middle 8

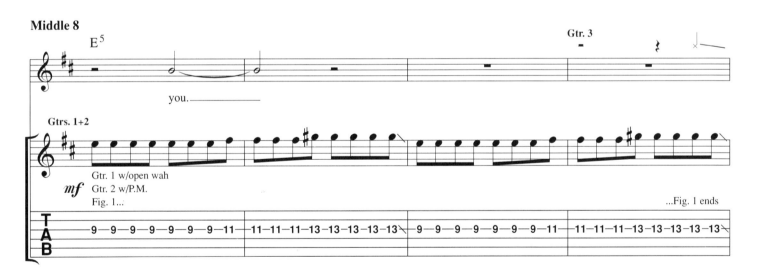

you._____

Gtrs. 1+2

Gtr. 1 w/open wah
Gtr. 2 w/P.M.
Fig. 1...:

...Fig. 1 ends

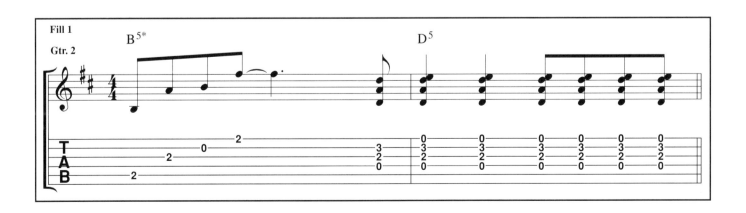

Fill 1
Gtr. 2

Chorus

But when you re - ly____ on a lie____ that's true,____

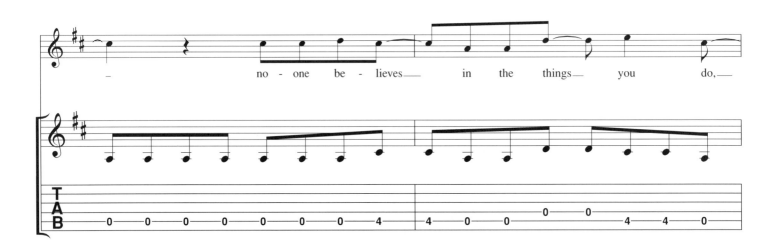

no - one be - lieves____ in the things____ you do,

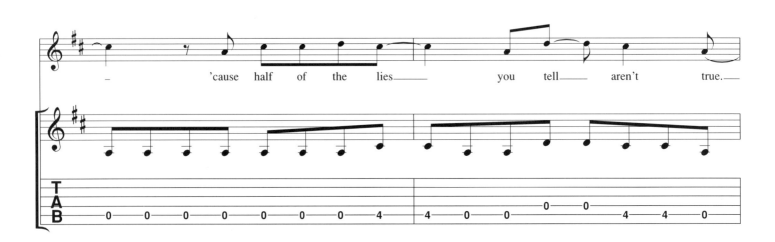

'cause half of the lies____ you tell____ aren't true.____

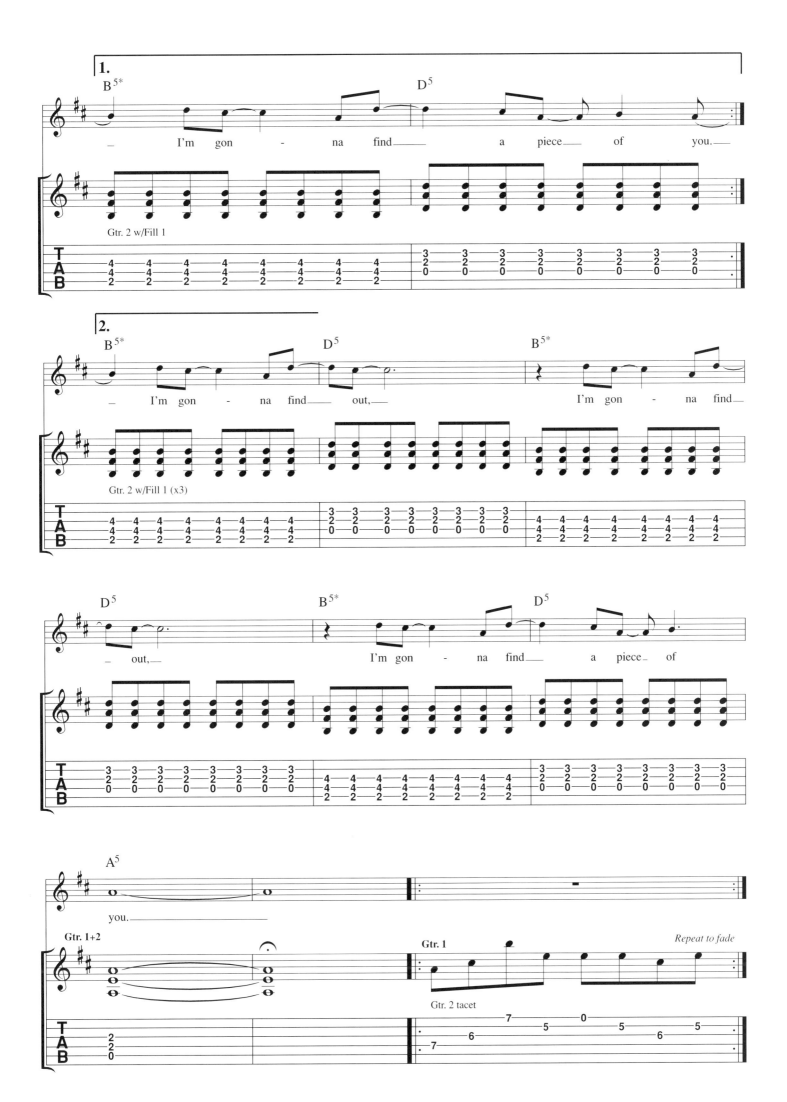

i wouldn't believe your radio

words by kelly jones
music by kelly jones, richard jones & stuart cable

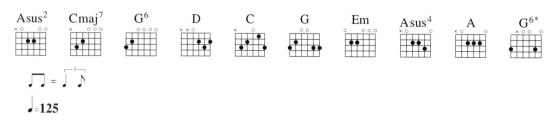

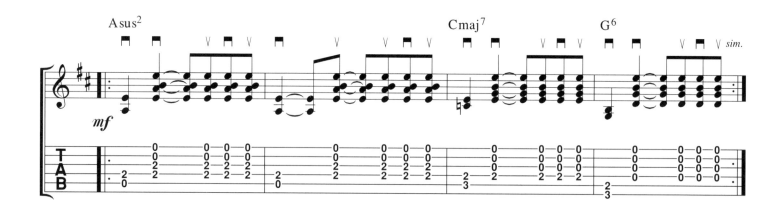

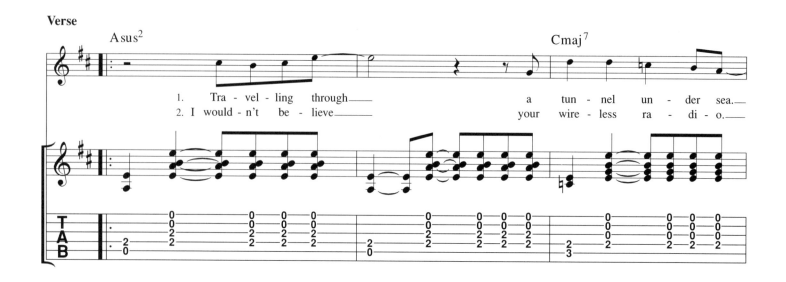

45

and you can pay for it the rest of your _____ li -

- - i - i - i - ife. _____

Li - - i - i - i - ife. _____

Gtr. 2 cont. in slashes

Guitar Solo

Gtrs. 1+2

Gtr. 3 (elec.)

w/dist. + slide
Fig. 2...

Gtrs. 1+2 w/Fig. 1 then cont. in slashes

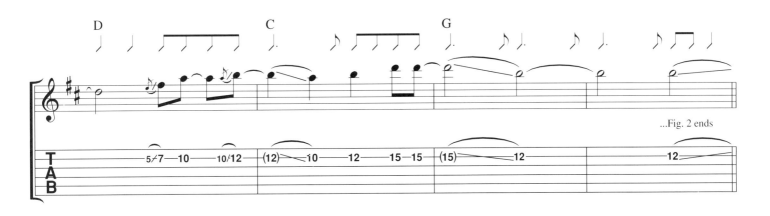

...Fig. 2 ends

Middle 8

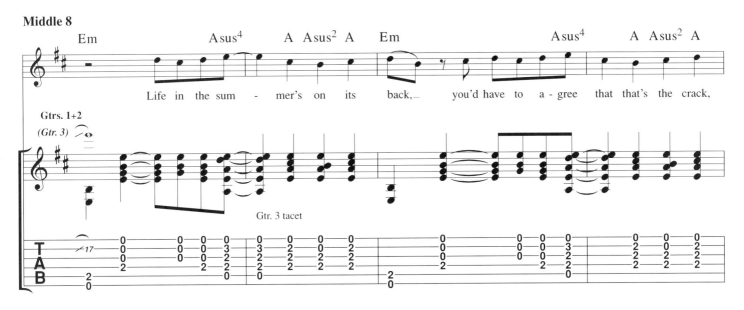

Life in the sum - mer's on its back,___ you'd have to a - gree that that's the crack,

Gtrs. 1+2
(Gtr. 3)

Gtr. 3 tacet

so take what you want___ I'm not co - ming back.___

Chorus

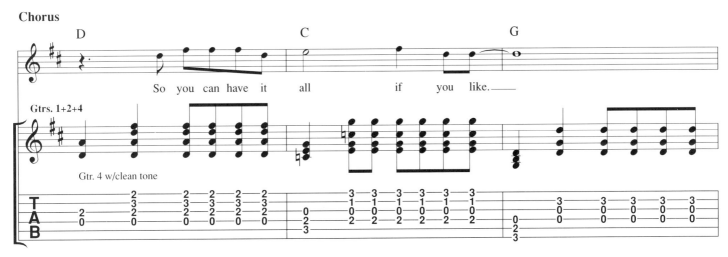

So you can have it all___ if you like.___

Gtrs. 1+2+4

Gtr. 4 w/clean tone

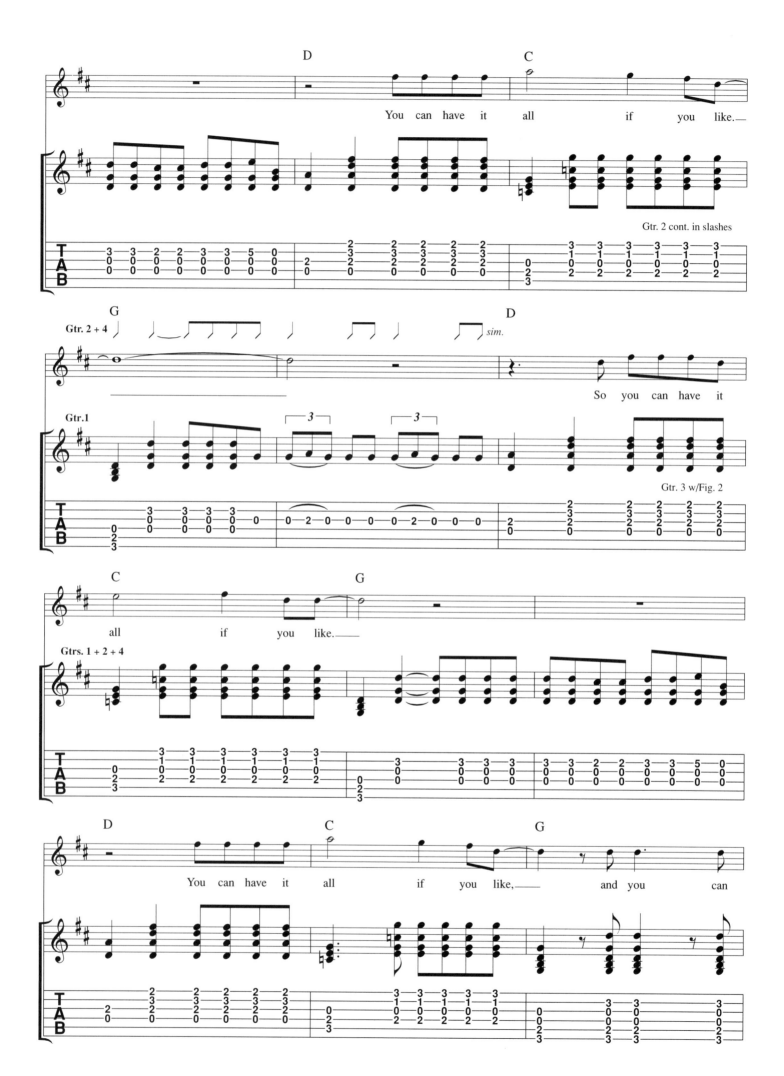

t-shirt suntan

words by kelly jones
music by kelly jones, richard jones & stuart cable

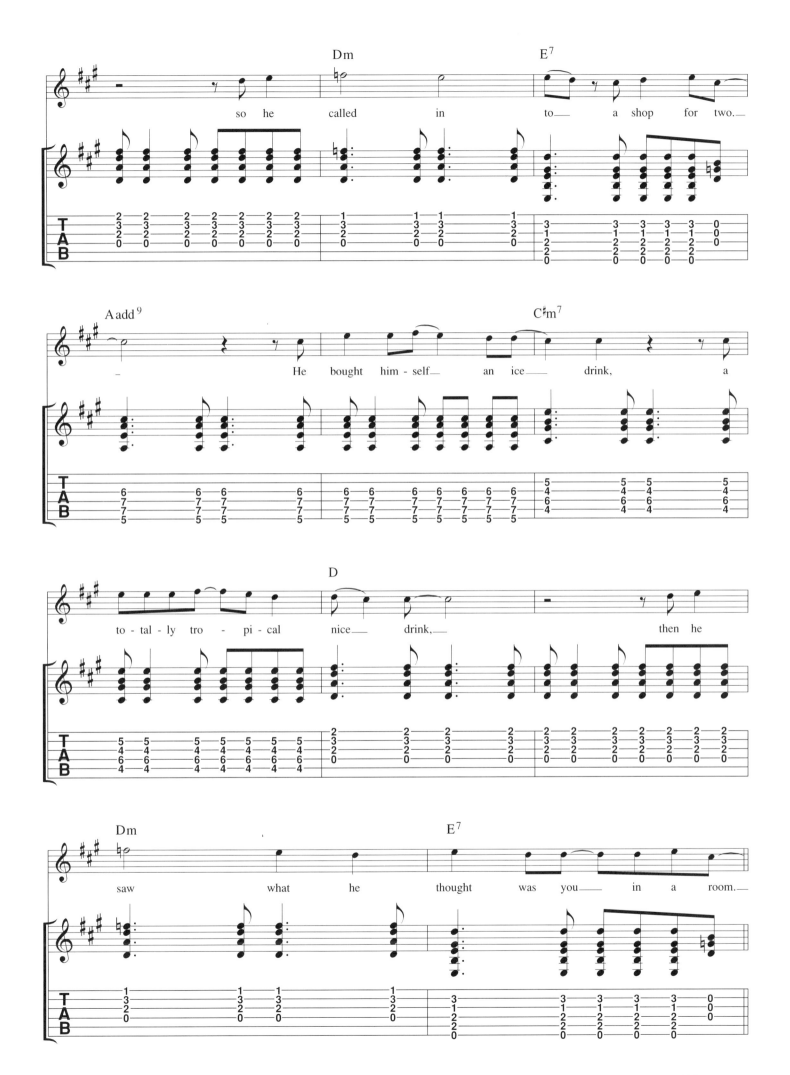

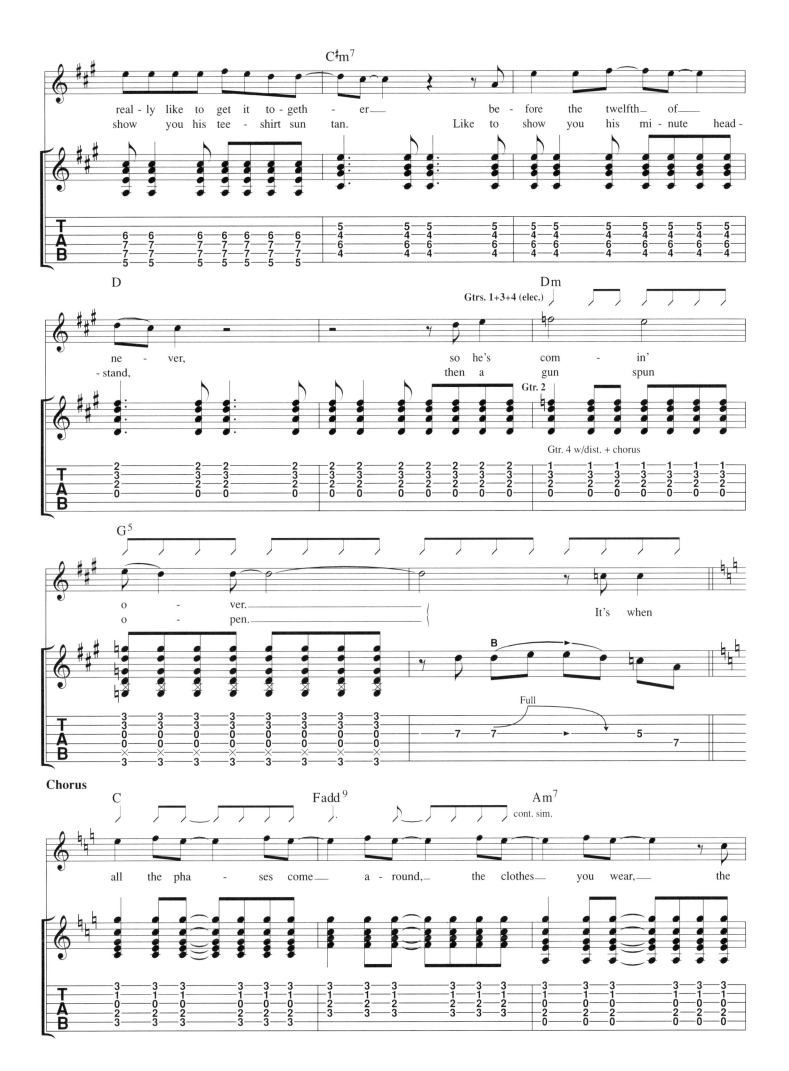

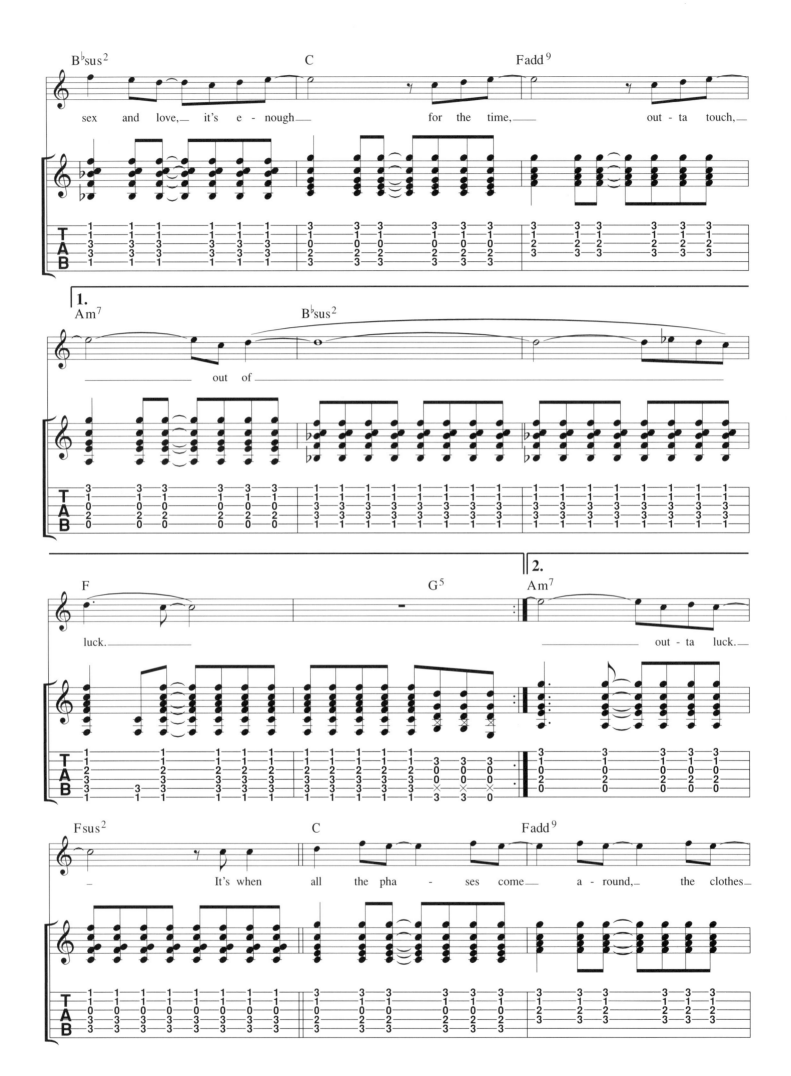

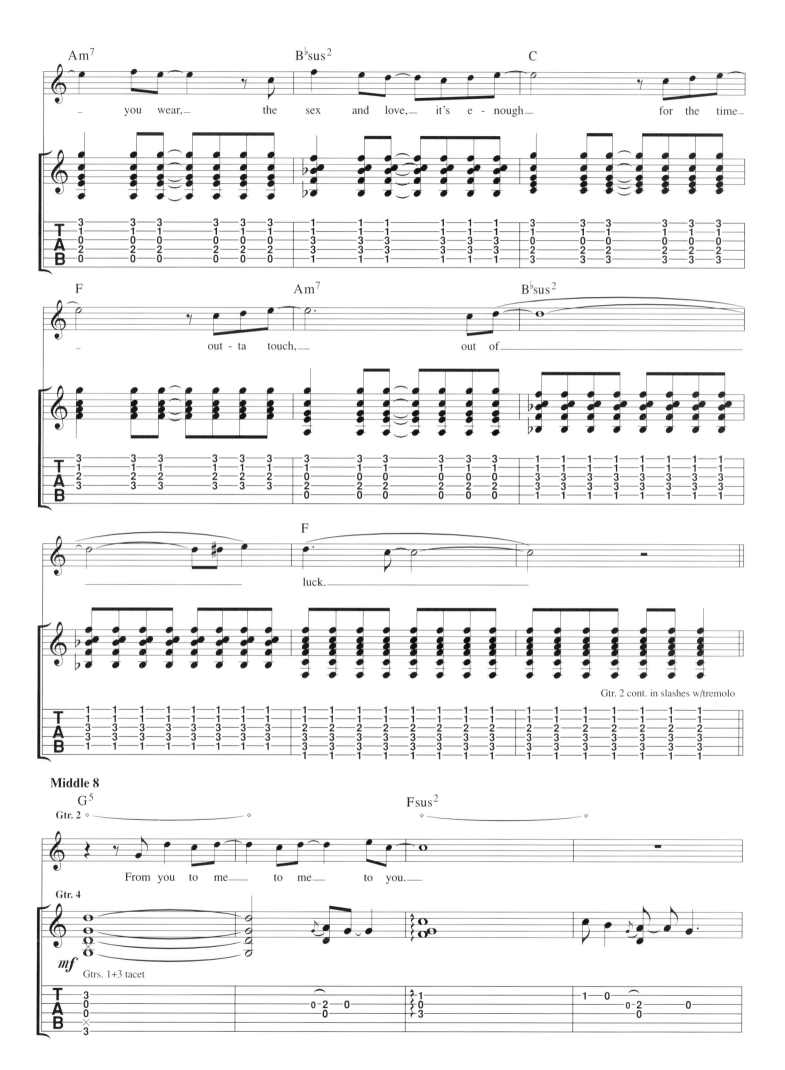

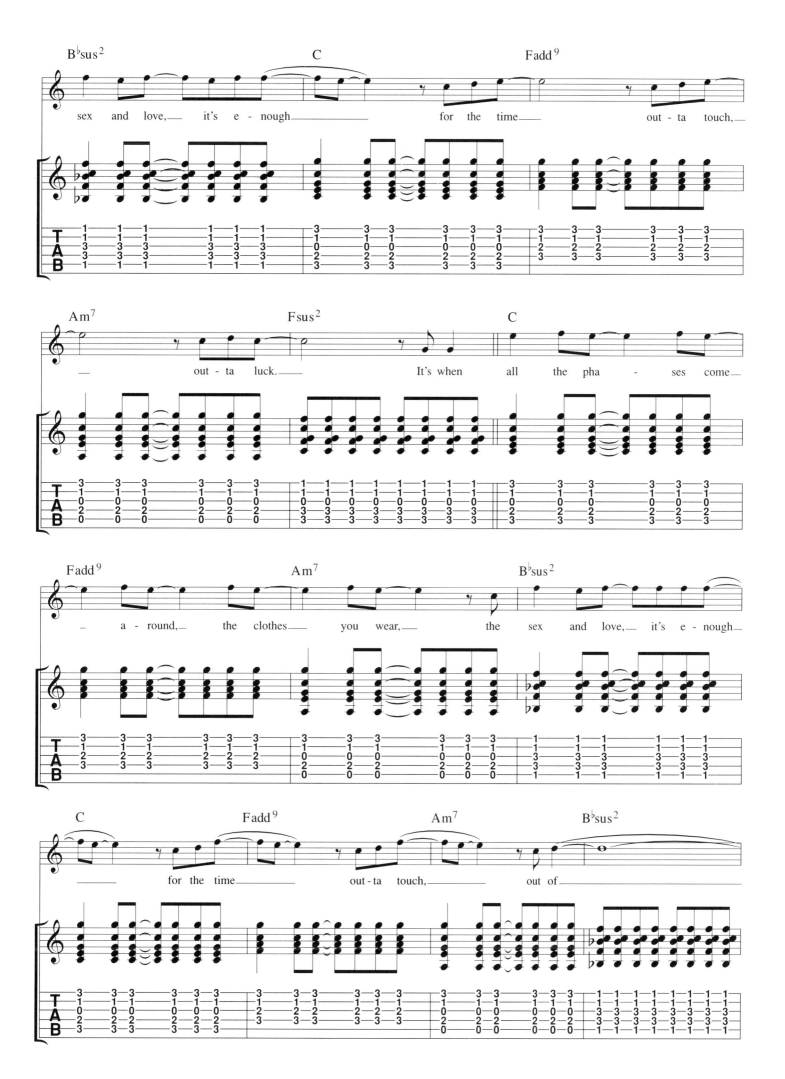

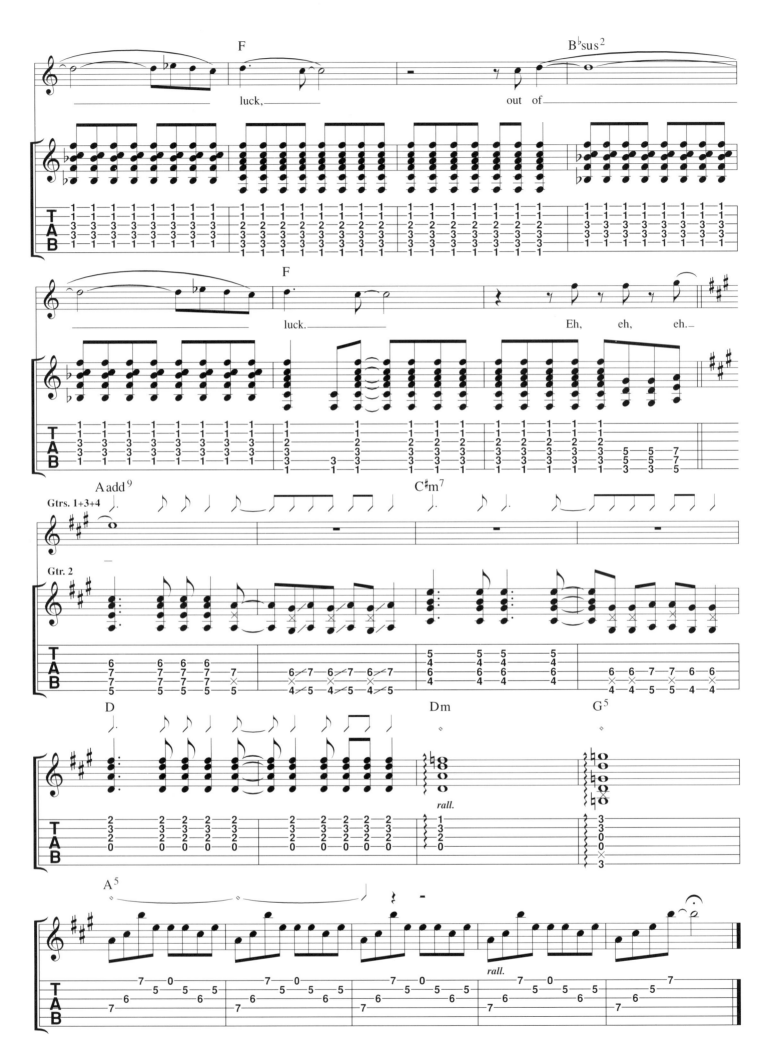

58

is yesterday, tomorrow, today?

words by kelly jones
music by kelly jones, richard jones & stuart cable

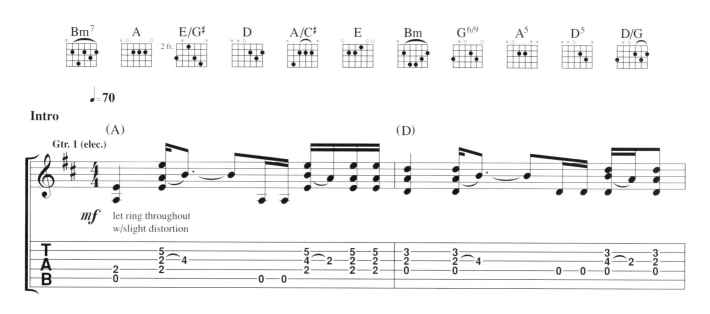

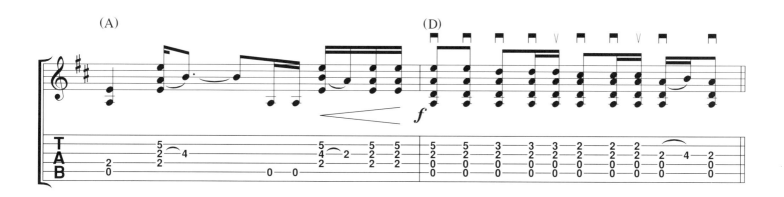

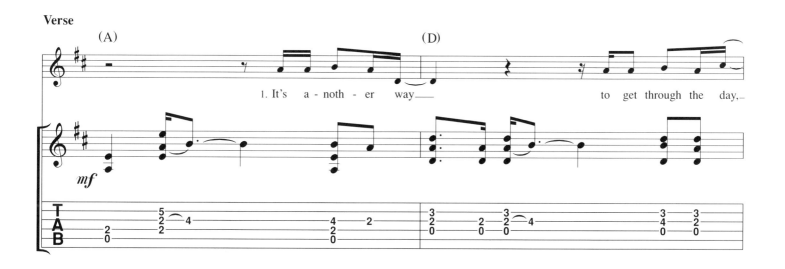

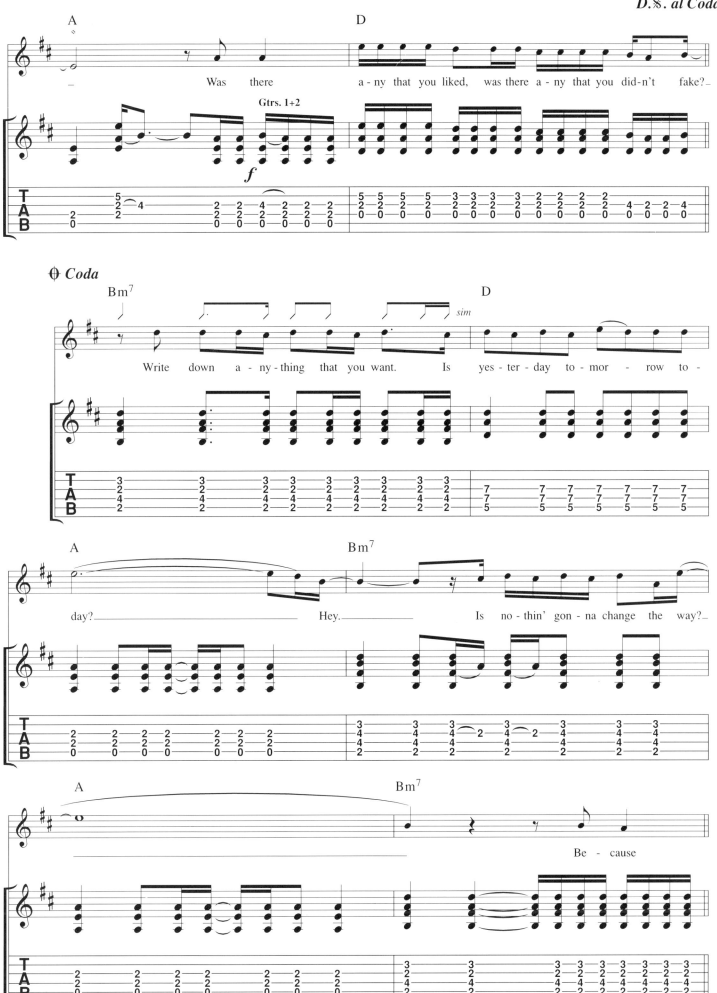

a minute longer

words by kelly jones
music by kelly jones, richard jones & stuart cable

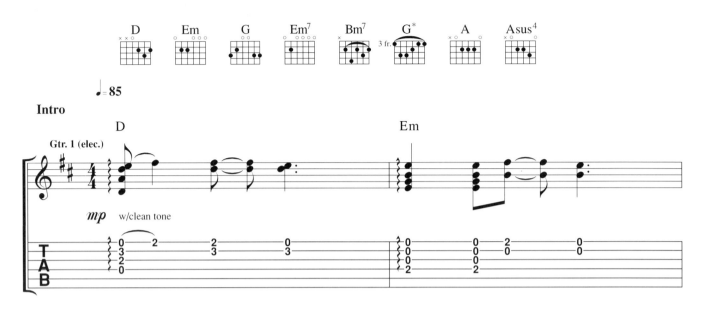

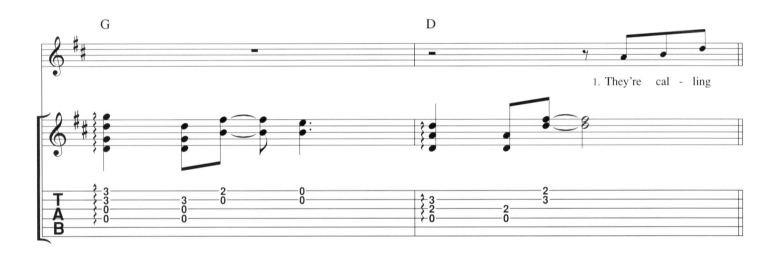

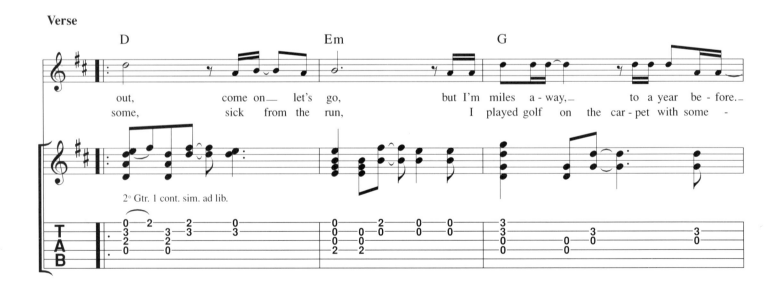

Chorus

she takes her clothes off

words by kelly jones
music by kelly jones, richard jones & stuart cable

plastic california

words by kelly jones
music by kelly jones, richard jones & stuart cable

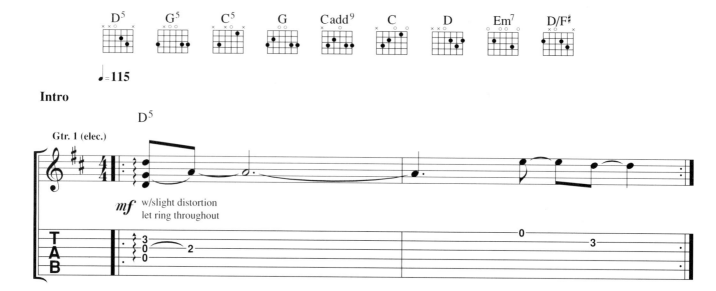

Intro

Verse

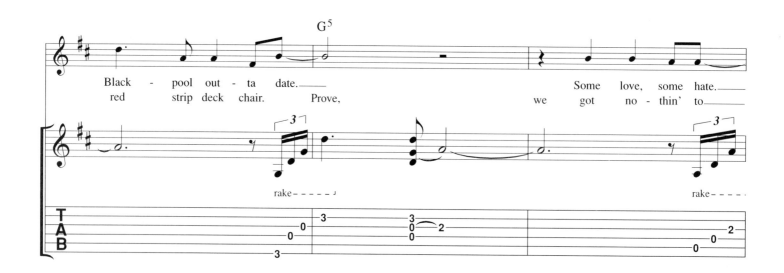

79

i stopped to fill my car up

words by kelly jones
music by kelly jones, richard jones & stuart cable

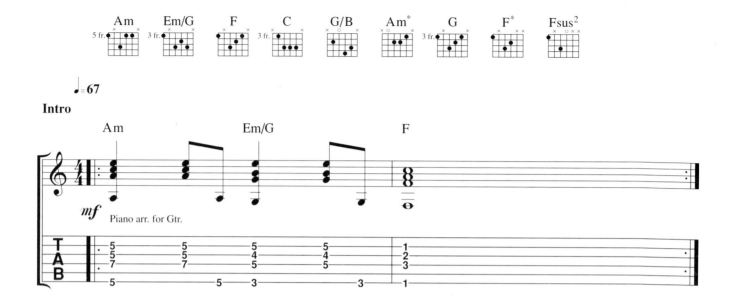

Intro

Verse

1. I stopped to fill my___ car___ up. The car felt___ good___ that___
2. A man round for - ty___ in the back___ seat. Must have stepped in when I was
(Verse 3 see block lyrics)

___ day.___ I did - n't know where___ I was go - ing,
em - pty.___ So why's he sat there___ just wait - ing,

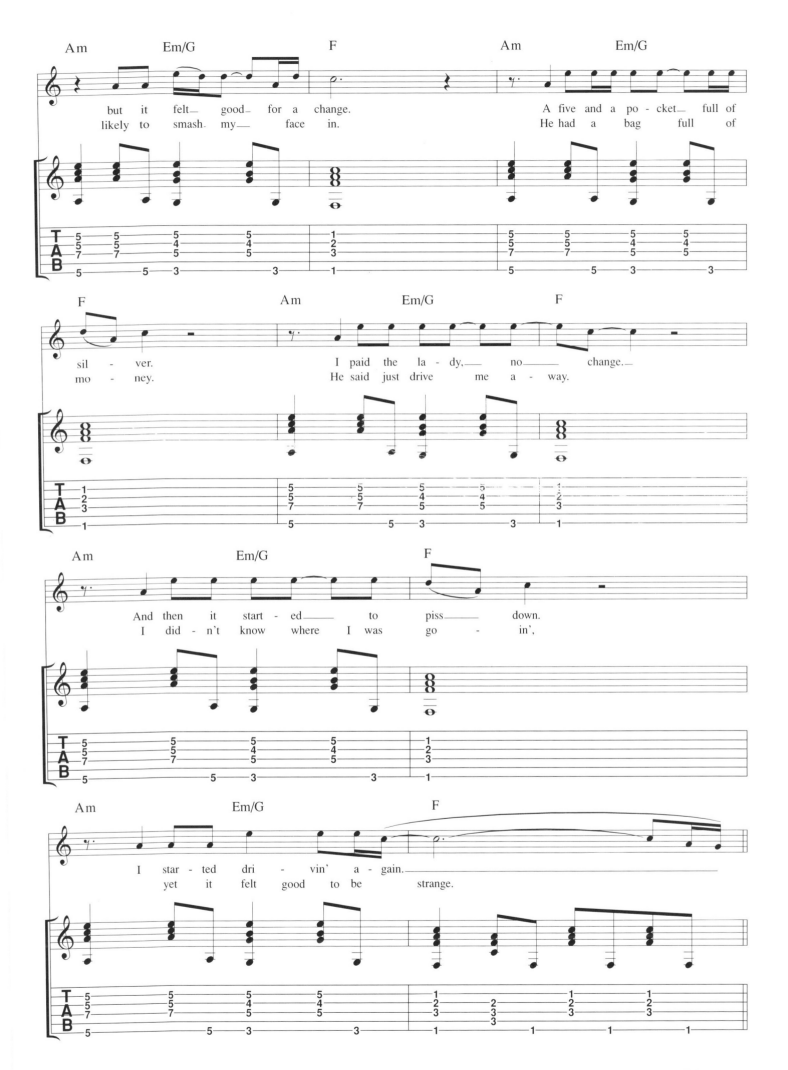

Chorus

Verse 3:

Curiosity is over
He stepped down from the car
He pulled a gun from his jacket
Said I was goin' to die.
It gives me so much satisfaction
To watch you beg and cry
I just made up this story
To get your attention
Makes me smile.

Chorus 3:

I never looked up
Or looked in
The mirror
Behind me
I never looked up
Or looked in
The mirror
Behind me.

4/00 (37050)